People of Passion

Stories of Faith and Determination That Will Touch Your Heart and Warm Your Soul

Spotlighting Southern Appalachia Representing America

Written & Compiled by Carl Mays

The Overmountain Press

JOHNSON CITY, TENNESSEE

Original cover painting, *Smoky Mountain Passion*,
by Vern Hippensteal

ISBN 1-57072-273-0
Copyright © 2004 by Carl Mays
Printed in the United States of America
All Rights Reserved

1 2 3 4 5 6 7 8 9 0

Table of Contents

Dedicated to the early Cherokees, mountaineers,
and highlanders who settled the Southern Appalachians and
contributed to the spirit of America

Introduction

In 1972, I came to East Tennessee and the Great Smoky Mountains on a six-month drama grant. Later, my work developed into that of a consultant and speaker to corporations and other groups. This career opened up to me the opportunity to travel throughout America as well as internationally, but Gatlinburg, Tennessee, has remained my home. I was captured by the beauty of the mountains and the surrounding area. I was also captured by the beauty and the heritage of the people living here. That's what led me to begin interviewing some of these people in 1974. I collected their stories and shared them with others through a newspaper column, some regional magazines, and orally.

Along with the interviews, I also researched the history of the Southern Highlands. This work helped me to fill in some gaps in the traditional stories, and it led to a greater appreciation of the vastness of the Appalachian range, which includes the Great Smoky Mountains.

Even though the early settlers of the Smokies region lived in isolation and developed a unique culture, the Appalachian Trail (completed in 1937) later brought some influences. With the trail, which extends over 2,000 miles from Mt. Katahdin, Maine, to Mt. Oglethorpe, Georgia, influences filtered down from New Hampshire's White Mountains and the Green Mountains of Vermont. The region gained some diversity from

New York's Catskills and Adirondacks, and the Alleghenies of Pennsylvania, Maryland, Virginia, West Virginia, and Kentucky. The Blue Ridge Mountains that stretch from Pennsylvania to Georgia, the Black Mountains of North Carolina, and the Unaka Mountains in Tennessee are all sisters and brothers with the Great Smoky Mountains of Tennessee and North Carolina.

As we consider the history of the people of the Southern Highlands, we acknowledge the early influence of the Cherokees. Some stories in this volume explore the lifestyles and struggles of these Native Americans, and tell of their conflicts with the early European settlers we now refer to as mountaineers and highlanders.

Many of these settlers were of Scotch-Irish descent. However, other peoples joined with these pioneers to carve places for themselves in history. Basically, the early settlers were simple, good-hearted people with faith in God, nature, themselves, and their neighbors. Though their legacy lives on, many of their stories are almost forgotten. That's why I wanted to reopen my files and revive some of their accounts in this book, a book I began over a quarter of a century ago.

These stories, which span a period of 200 years, concentrate on a certain region of the nation. They demonstrate the principles, the spirit, and the character of the people upon which our nation has been built.

Some of these stories may surprise you. Some may elicit a smile or cause you to laugh aloud. Others may bring a lump to your throat, or tears to your eyes. Some may simply cause you to look up from the pages for a few moments and think about the courage, sacrifices, and contributions of these early Americans.

I can't predict your reaction to these profiles and chronicles, but I do know that the people of these stories and these mountains represent well every American who has paid a price for "life, liberty, and the pursuit of happiness."

—Carl Mays

The Father of Tennessee

In the mid-1700s, some inhabitants of eastern North Carolina grew restless. Their restlessness led them westward, into what is now the state of Tennessee. Traveling over the part of the Appalachians that was to become known as the Great Smoky Mountains, the people liked what they found. Soon, news of "the land of milk and honey" spread.

The word reached William Bean in Virginia. In 1768, he made the southwest trek and fell in love with the territory. Stopping northeast of the Smoky Mountains, he cleared some land and built a cabin in the Watauga River Valley, near what today is the Roan Mountain and Boone's Creek region. The following year, Bean returned to Virginia for his family and a small group of friends. Overcoming great odds, these people traveled to settle in the area, bringing a tinge of civilization to a small speck of this beautiful but challenging wilderness.

It has been indicated that Daniel Boone led an official expedition out of Kentucky in 1769 to inspect the territory that would later be named Tennessee. Coming by way of the Cumberland Gap, west of where Bean had entered the territory, Boone and his explorers were highly impressed with the region. They traveled on into North Carolina, where they shared with others the details of the virgin territory filled with green growth and abundant game.

James Robertson was among the Carolinians to hear the

descriptive stories that were passed around. Shortly thereafter, this Scotch-Irishman traveled to the new land to see if what Daniel Boone and his group said was really true. Discovering the beauty of the mountains and valleys for himself, Robertson quickly decided to return to North Carolina and bring his family with him to settle in this land of promise.

James Robertson, however, was no Daniel Boone. He was unaccustomed to exploring in such uncharted areas and in finding his way through the wilderness of this strange territory. His excitement and eagerness to return to his family with the good news was much greater than his sense of direction. Robertson became lost in the Great Smoky Mountains. With only his horse as a companion, he searched frantically for something to guide him through the steep and densely covered terrain, but to no avail. Soon, he lost his horse. Later, his food was gone and he became exhausted. He was freezing, and his hope for survival was close to being completely extinguished.

The lack of food, the exhaustion, and the frantic, desperate desire for self-preservation brought Robertson to his knees, physically and spiritually. He prayed. Then he collapsed. As the story goes, James Robertson was more dead than alive when four hunters happened upon his lifeless form. Three of the hunters said Robertson was too far gone to revive, but the fourth man refused to accept their decision. As a result of this man's actions, Robertson was saved.

James Robertson eventually reunited with his family in North Carolina. After recuperating from his ordeal, he led his family and a group of followers back into the beautiful land where he had almost lost his life. William Bean greeted Robertson and his band with these words: "I desire you to make my home your home. From this moment, as long as it is convenient to you, you are members of my family."

Such sentiment on the part of Bean greatly impressed Robertson, and it stuck with him as he became one of the leaders of the new settlement. The hospitality shown him by Bean, and the kindness and concern of the hunter who brought him back to life, became inherent parts of Robertson. These qualities led him to become one of the five commissioners called for by the first free and independent government in America. Established in 1772 and called the Watauga Association, this new democratic government was formed at a time when the thirteen colonies were still under British rule.

These early Tennesseans, led by men like Robertson, were to do much to remove such rule. Robertson eventually pushed farther westward, where he helped settle Nashville, and he earned the name of "The Father of Tennessee."

The Most Notable of the Cherokee Chiefs

John Ross was born in 1790, near Lookout Mountain, Tennessee. His father was a successful Scottish trader who saw to it that Ross had the best of tutors and access to a private school. Ross went on to receive his college degree in Maryville, Tennessee. So how was it, with his privileged background, that John Ross became the most notable of the Cherokee chiefs?

To gain more insight into this improbable situation, we scour historical records to discover that Ross's grandfather came to America as a British agent among the Cherokees. He eventually married a young woman who was half Cherokee. Thus, John Ross was born one-eighth Cherokee. However, it was still highly unlikely that this man would become a Cherokee chief and remain in such a position for nearly forty years. He served as a principal chief longer than any other Native American in history.

Following the Revolutionary War, the newly formed United States government did not have enough money to pay its soldiers. Without money, the government paid in acreage, including land in the Southern Appalachian region, if the recipients would take it. During the war, the Cherokees had been swayed by the British to fight against the rebellious colonists. The settlers felt that the Cherokees had forfeited their rights to the land as a result of their alliance and ultimate defeat with the British.

Even though John Ross was more "white" than "red," his heart ached when he saw how the Cherokees were being pushed from their homeland. Having "mixed blood," he did not want to see one group of people gain at the expense of another. He knew that the Cherokees could live and work side by side with the whites. Like the new Americans, the Cherokees were farmers. They lived in log cabins rather than tepees or wigwams. They were not nomadic, but instead wanted to put down stakes.

In fact, the Cherokees had put down stakes years earlier. They were farming when De Soto encountered them in the Great Smoky Mountains in 1540. Almost three centuries later, in 1825, the great Cherokee Sequoyah combined letters from various European languages to create a Cherokee alphabet. Soon thereafter, most Cherokees could read and write their language. A newspaper, the *Cherokee Phoenix*, followed.

Christian missionaries made inroads into Cherokee culture, and the Cherokees established their own schools and churches. However, the rush for land by European settlers was causing many conflicts, which Ross tried valiantly to stop. Because he devoted his life to bring peace between the clashing cultures, the Cherokees gave him the name of *Gu'wisguwi'*, meaning "large white bird."

While the battles continued in the Southern Highlands, Ross spent much of his time in Washington, D.C., attempting to design treaties and draw up workable solutions that would allow the settlers and the Native Americans to live in peace. Time and again, however, he was disappointed. The Cherokees were first driven from North Carolina, then from Tennessee in 1828, going on to settle in the area of Head of Coosa (later Rome), Georgia.

At Head of Coosa John Ross became a planter, building a large plantation. Since much of his time was spent in Washington, most of the work was done by a vast number of black slaves. Ironically, while Ross tirelessly toiled to free the Cherokees from the white man's dominion, many whites were laboring unceasingly to free blacks from the bondage of both whites and Cherokees.

Ross was in Washington in 1830, where he received word that the Cherokees were being pushed off their territory in Georgia. By the time he arrived home, his entire plantation had been confiscated by soldiers and other whites. Remaining loyal to the United States government, Ross refused to fight. Instead, he moved north of Rome to Rossville, a town named earlier in his honor. Ross had previously lived in Rossville in a a two-story log house his grandfather McDonald had built in 1797, and now he returned to the area and made it his new home.

Then, as if his disappointments with the U.S. government were not bad enough, he was betrayed by some of his fellow Cherokees. To get more money for their land, which they believed would inevitably go to the U.S. government anyway, these traitors signed an unauthorized treaty signifying that all Cherokees would move from the East.

Ross moved his family from Georgia back to Tennessee, settling in Red Clay, an ancient Cherokee council place. He split time between living there with his family in a small cabin and trying to work with the president, congress, the Indian commissioner, and the Supreme Court in Washington.

In 1834, Ross said, "Our existence as an independent nation is drawing to a close." By 1838, John Ross knew that the Cherokees would be pushed from the East. In April of that year, Ross personally negotiated with President Van Buren regarding the removal terms, but even these agreements were not kept. In the winter of 1838-1839, the Cherokees were hastily and unceremoniously forced out of their homeland.

Marching westward, the ones who survived the trip did not stop until they ended up in Oklahoma, a journey of 1200 miles. Labeled the "Trail of Tears," the march is said to have taken the lives of from 4,000 to 20,000 Cherokees. The exact number is debated because of the unorganized manner in which the Cherokees were evicted. John Ross's own wife, a Cherokee named Quatie, died along the way.

Meanwhile, some of the Cherokees, among them a leader named Tsali, escaped the march and hid out in the Great Smoky Mountains. They scavenged for food and shelter, becoming even more bitter enemies with many of the whites who settled the land. Eventually, this band of approximately 1000 Cherokees was assisted by whites who believed in what John Ross had been trying to accomplish. These sympathizers organized to purchase about 60,000 acres of land and gave it to the Cherokees. Today, the area encompasses Cherokee, North Carolina, and is still privately owned by the tribe.

John Ross and the survivors of the group he led west joined with four other Native American nations in eastern Oklahoma. His people became the leaders, and John Ross was named Principal Chief of the Cherokee Nation, in both the West and the East. He never ceased fighting for Native American rights.

While in Washington on August 1, 1886, in the midst of a mission, John Ross died at the age of seventy-six. The prediction he made in 1834, that the Cherokees' existence as an independent nation was doomed, came true in 1906, when the Cherokees became citizens of the United States.

The memory of the faith, dedication, and loyalty of John Ross still serves to make him a hero to all people who have a dream—to people who still work for a peaceful existence among all God's creatures.

The Blankets Are Joined!

Even though there were three distinct Cherokee dialects and seven clans living in forty-three villages, when young adult Cherokees were ready to marry, there was an established basic tradition they followed.

In this tradition, a young Cherokee named Sharro readied himself to call upon his betrothed, Sehoya. He began by tracking down a deer, the most magnificent he could find. Within distance of his prey, he silently asked for permission to kill the animal. Cherokees never killed animals for sport, realizing that every creature of the life chain has a purpose. Sensing permission given, Sharro took aim and brought the animal down with a single arrow.

Sharro then dressed the deer, taking specific parts for specific purposes. Two of the pieces went to his brothers and sisters. One went to his neighbors, who had helped take care of his family since the death of his mother and father. The loins were prepared for presentation to Sehoya.

The remainder of the carcass was left for the wolves. A Cherokee would never kill wolves and, when possible, would leave food for them. Cherokees believed wolves were messengers of the spirit world. Elders often listened to the wolves' lonely howls to gain insight and wisdom. Sharro wanted to insure additional hope for the success of his marriage by sharing his prize catch with the wolves.

Sharro packed the chosen meat in the deerskin and carried it back to the village. He visited with his younger brothers and sisters and then with the neighbors, before washing up, changing clothes, and leaving at dusk with the loins to call upon Sehoya.

Sharro arrived unannounced, stopped outside Sehoya's home, and called out to her mother. When Sehoya's mother appeared at the entranceway, Sharro silently offered the gift to her. At once, she knew the significance of this special gift and accepted it gladly.

Sehoya's mother stepped back inside. Then Sehoya stepped out, moving shyly, not allowing Sharro to see her eyes, and invited him into the cabin. He sat and watched as Sehoya, coached and coaxed by her proud mother, cooked a piece of the best part of the tenderloin for Sharro to eat. In the shadows, her younger brothers and sisters watched, whispered, and giggled with delight. Every now and then, Sehoya, with her eyes down, would glance shyly toward Sharro, allowing herself a nervous smile. Cooking the meat for Sharro meant that she accepted him as her husband-to-be.

Later, the couple visited a village shaman. He sat them down and performed a tobacco ceremony, testing for the presence of witches or other afflictions that might corrupt the marriage. Sharro and Sehoya were pronounced acceptable as partners.

Upon the approval of the shaman, Sharro's male friends treated him to a ceremonial meal. During this time of celebration and frivolity, his friends passed along hints and tips for his wedding night. They warned him of the awkwardness he would experience. Everyone knew that Sehoya was a high-spirited, beautiful young lady. They also knew that she had always been properly chaperoned and protected. They knew that this would be the "first time" for both Sharro and Sehoya.

Meanwhile, Sehoya was also being feted. Much more quietly, she was treated to her favorite foods and was waited on by other young ladies who were not yet married. Even though happy, the occasion was rather solemn and reflective.

Upon completion of the dinners, the male guests walked into the council house and lined up on one side. The females then entered and stood across from them. Attendants led Sharro into the house and stood with him. With her attendants, Sehoya was escorted to the other side of the room. Sharro's mother was dead, so one of his aunts brought him a venison roast and a blanket, gifts for sustenance and comfort. Sehoya's mother then gave her an ear of corn and a blanket.

The relatives returned to their places, leaving Sharro standing across from Sehoya. Slowly, the two approached one another. She daringly looked into his eyes now, and he into hers. Sharro extended his blanket toward Sehoya. She accepted it and very carefully folded it with her own. She then gave him her corn, and he handed her the roast. The village's main chief came forward to joyously announce, "The blankets are joined!"

The Value of Religion

There is no way to judge the value of religion except by what it does. That's what Caleb Porter believed. That's the standard by which he lived, in the Southern Highlands, in the early 1800s. Caleb wasn't an ordained minister. He was a farmer, but people said he had been touched by the Lord. Those who knew him best claimed that he, more than anyone else, understood the meaning of living and dying. They said he was unique in the way he related to other people and to God. That's why the entire countryside was up in arms when Caleb met with his tragedy.

Caleb, his wife, and their son lived near an isolated fort, when Cherokees attacked that stronghold. The battle was part of what was known later as the "Cherokee War." Following the battle at the fort, four of the Cherokees broke away from the war party and laid siege to Caleb's home. Caleb was away at the time, but his wife and son were not. Seeking revenge for past defeats at the hands of the whites, the marauders raped Caleb's wife, scalped her alive, and then decapitated her. The boy was tied to a tree; his arms and legs were severed from his body, and then he was burned.

Caleb went into shock when he and his friends returned home. His companions promised him they would round up everyone in the area to form a posse. They swore to capture the raiders responsible for the torture and death of Caleb's family.

Caleb did not visibly respond to their promises. When the men departed, Caleb confined himself to his home. For days, he saw and spoke with no one. He ate nothing and slept little as his initial shock gave way to fasting, praying, and reading the Bible.

Within nine days, the posse returned. The men were tired, almost to the point of exhaustion, but Caleb knew they had been successful in capturing the marauders. He could tell by the men's voices as they called to him from outside the cabin. A deep silence prevailed when Caleb opened the cabin door and stepped out to see the Cherokees who had massacred his wife and son. Some of the posse had wanted to kill the prisoners as soon as they were caught. The majority, however, decided they should be brought back. It was agreed that Caleb should witness their deaths.

The captives refused to look at the man who walked from the cabin they knew so well. With assistance from some of the posse, however, the Cherokees were finally forced to look into Caleb's eyes. A long silence followed.

"I forgive them," Caleb said softly, much more softly than the usual voice coming from this giant of a man. "Killing them will not bring back my wife and son. It will not erase the grief." The men of the posse could not believe what they heard. The look on Caleb's face told them he meant exactly what he said.

Caleb looked at the posse. One by one, he thanked them for the sacrifice and dedication they had offered him. Then he said, "Christ instructs us in Matthew 5:44 to 'Love your enemies, bless them that curse you, do good to them that hate you, and pray for them which despitefully use you, and persecute you.'"

The posse looked at the captives, at one another, then back toward Caleb as he spoke. "It is hate that has led us to where we are today," he said. Caleb asked some of the posse to free the prisoners' wrists, which were tied behind their backs.

Then, in silence, Caleb took the reins of the Cherokees' horses and handed them to the captives. The Cherokees did not move. Caleb said, "Go," and gestured with his hands, palms upward.

The Cherokees stood still. Then, slowly, one by one, they slid from their mounts and knelt at Caleb's feet. As they bowed before him, placing their lives in his hands, they sensed the presence of God, even though they had no concept of the fullness of His form and nature. Later, Caleb taught them such concepts.

Brave Women

The region's "Cherokee War," along with the unrest leading up to and following it, resulted in years filled with fear and bitterness on both sides. As a result, there were many exploits that entitled the women of the Great Smoky Mountains area to become known as heroines.

One woman lost her husband in the war but resisted all pleas to move herself and her two small children into a fort. Instead, she held fast to the property she and her husband had settled. There, she scooped out a bed for her children under the floor of her cabin and stood guard over them, night after night, with a loaded rifle. Finally, in admiration of her courage, the Cherokees would pass by her cabin on their midnight raids, leaving her to farm her little clearing in safety.

Another woman, known as Esther, showed her bravery when she, her husband, and her children were surrounded late at night by a band of approximately twenty-five Cherokees. In the cabin, Esther and her husband heard a noise coming from the nearby stables. Not realizing anyone was on the premises, the husband ventured outside to investigate the disturbance. He was shot down and scalped by the intruders.

Fearing the worst after hearing the gunshots, Esther locked the door and stood by the entrance with a rifle in her hand. There, surrounded by her sleeping children, she waited in silent expectation. Soon, she heard approaching footsteps.

Was it her husband? Was it the distant neighbors, aroused by the noise, coming to the rescue? Esther's questions quickly received a negative answer when she heard voices speaking Cherokee. The truth flashed upon her—her husband had been killed, and she was left to defend herself and her children against a group of enraged avengers who would delight in her torture.

Esther caught her breath but made no audible sound as she grasped the rifle and pointed it toward the locked door. The footsteps drew nearer, and the voices became louder. Suddenly, the door was jolted by a heavy force. The wooden bolt on the door flexed, and the door itself partly opened. One intruder fell to his knees and stuck his arm through the opening. Another grabbed the door at its middle. Still another pushed from the top.

Esther had only recently learned to shoot a rifle, but she instantly pulled the trigger. The man at the bottom of the door yelled with pain as he withdrew his arm. The other two men ceased their break-in attempt, surprised at the defense and anxious to check on their wounded cohort.

Meanwhile, Esther reloaded as quickly as she could. Then the two unscathed intruders resumed their barrage. Esther fired again, this time hitting the man pushing on the center of the door. He yelled and fell backward with a thud. The third warrior didn't wait around to give Esther another chance. He and the rest of the band hurriedly gathered their wounded companion and the dead man and fled from the range of Esther's rifle.

The heroines during the pioneer period were by no means only white women. The account of a Cherokee maiden known as White Fawn attests to this fact.

White Fawn was captured when a group of white men on a rampage almost completely destroyed her village late one evening with a surprise attack. Most of the inhabitants of the village were killed or dispersed, but the young and attractive

White Fawn was one of the few spared and taken prisoner.

The victorious group and the prisoners had been back from the raid for only a couple of days, however, when Abe Miller's leg began to turn black and swell to twice its normal size. Abe was the leader of the attackers, and he had injured his leg during the attack on the village. There was no doctor nearby, and no one in the encampment knew what to do. Abe became worse, dropping into unconsciousness with a high fever. That's when White Fawn volunteered to take matters into her own hands.

The Cherokee maiden waited until the swelling in the leg reached a certain point, then she decided the time was right for lancing the wound. With a sharp knife, she cut into the darkened flesh. She then instructed the other men to provide her with boiling water and clean rags. The swelling began to subside, and the color began to return to normal, as Abe's fever broke and he regained consciousness. White Fawn fed him with a special soup made from roots and herbs she had instructed the other men to gather. Within a week after the operation, it was evident that Abe was going to recover completely.

White Fawn gained the respect and admiration of everyone in the encampment. They all knew she easily could have let Abe Miller suffer and die, just as they had caused the people of her village to suffer and die. But she had chosen to help a man she detested, simply because he was in need of help.

White Fawn and the other captives were allowed to go free. Within that group of white men, White Fawn's courageous act of kindness did much to change their thinking about the Cherokees.

The Miracle of Giving

The early settlers of the Southern Highlands were an independent breed who loved the outdoors and loved to live. They loved to breathe the fresh mountain air, to hunt and wander at will in the thick forests, while carving out foothill farms. Because of the nature of these pioneers, stories such as the ones in this volume have been passed on to their descendants. This oral tradition accounts for the abundance of tales that have made the rounds in the Southern Appalachians for so many years.

Like us, these early mountaineers were far from perfect, but beautiful, inspiring stories have come from their experiences as they adapted to the struggle for survival and sought to find meaning and fulfillment in life. I've heard several versions of this story I share with you now. I've been told that it has spread far beyond the Southern Appalachian region. Some people claim it's not really true, that it's just a fable with a moral. Others tell me it is definitely true, and that their grandparents swore by it. The story involves a woman named Hattie Whaley.

Hattie, a tall, strong, mountain woman, is said to have lived with her husband and three small children in a cabin on a foothills farm in the early 1800s. At times, her husband would go away for two or three days to do some trading and get supplies. Hattie was left alone with the children while he was gone. The woman was almost isolated; her nearest neighbors were over three miles away.

Being left alone didn't frighten Hattie. There were always the threats of wild animals and unfriendly vagabonds, but she did what she had to do. Such was her task on that particular morning in July when her husband departed on one of his trips.

He wasn't out of sight before Hattie was in the garden behind her cabin, wanting to do the hoeing before the sun climbed any higher. The children were still asleep, and this gave her an extra incentive to get on with the job.

Hattie had stroked only a few rows of weeds with her hoe when her chore was abruptly ended. With lightning quickness, before she realized what had happened, the scaly head of a disturbed timber rattler sprang from behind her and sank its fangs into the back of her leg. Hattie quickly whirled around and retaliated with the sharp hoe. The large snake was dead, but Hattie knew she was, too. The fatal poison from this dreaded, dangerous species was already in her bloodstream.

Hattie thought of running for help, but no one was around, except for the faraway neighbors. Her husband, with their only horse pulling the wagon, had been gone too long for her to catch up with him. Hattie knew the more she moved, the sooner she would die. She then thought of the children. They were too young to do anything to help—the oldest was only five.

Suddenly, Hattie realized she would die, and the children would be left by themselves. In her mind's eye, she could see her husband returning and finding all of them dead. Thinking no more of her own impending death, Hattie ran to the children and awakened them. She grabbed the two smaller ones in her arms and told the five-year-old to follow her. Without hesitation, she began running to the closest neighbor's farm.

Hattie grew faint and weak as she ran. She became sicker with each step, but she stopped only twice, to submit to the churning of her stomach. The five-year-old, unable to keep pace, climbed up on Hattie's back after the second stop.

Finally, Hattie neared Ben Huskey's farm. Ben was out in his field plowing, when he looked up and saw a gripping scene. On one hand and her knees, Hattie was crawling into a clearing. In her other arm she held a baby; the second baby clung to her back. The five-year-old was walking beside her.

Hattie's face, arms, and legs were covered with blood, where branches and briars had struck her as she ran, walked, and, finally, crawled for help. Her clothing was drenched with sweat, which still gushed from her in great rivulets.

The children were saved, and so was Hattie. Ben Huskey said she lived as a result of all the tremendous exertion and the almost unbelievable amount of perspiration washing the poison from her body. Some people disagreed with Huskey. They claimed it was a miracle—the type of miracle that happens when people place the lives of others before their own.

Freedom for All

Early America was much like Europe in that there were primarily two classes of people: an aristocratic class of business and land owners, and the working class. The enterprising middle class had not yet established itself. The aristocrats grabbed up the fertile lands near the east coast, using the mild climate, navigable streams, and good harbors to facilitate direct trade with Europe. In the South, the system of large plantations limited the number of Americans who could actively prosper under such conditions.

Thus, as the aristocrats remained near the shore, other hardy Europeans accepted the challenge of the high mountain ranges, moving west to establish something of their own. Scotch-Irish and Germans, along with some Huguenots, Quakers, and poor English who had served their time as indentured servants in the East made the trek to find better opportunities for themselves and their families. Many of these people settled first in the mountainous regions of Pennsylvania and Maryland. Later, they moved on down to the Shenandoah Valley of Virginia.

Eventually, the Shenandoah Valley became a channel for a continuous movement of people passing through, moving south into the Carolinas, Kentucky, Tennessee, and Georgia. The process accelerated as eastern aristocrats determined that enslaving Africans was more profitable and productive than the system of European indentured servitude. As slavery increased, more and more indentured servants were freed to find independence to the south and beyond the mountains.

Therefore, it should come as no surprise that an antislavery sentiment grew among the mountaineers who struggled to establish an individualistic way of life. These were people who had come from unsettled conditions in Europe during its devastating wars of the seventeenth and eighteenth centuries. They had fled to America to pursue political liberty and religious freedom, among other reasons.

Antislavery groups began to form in areas comprised of whites whose families had personally experienced the effects of servitude. One such group was the North Carolina Manumission Society. The society denounced the importation and exportation of slaves, and, as the name implies, they provided for the purchase of slave contracts to help the slaves gain freedom. The influence of the society was considerable, evidenced by the fact that one of its members was elected to the state Senate in 1826. Through the society's efforts, over 2,000 slaves in North Carolina were freed between 1824-1826.

Between 1817-1830, some Baptist ministers in the mountains of Tennessee and Kentucky joined forces to promote and encourage emancipation. They maintained that there should be no fellowship with slaveholders. Without a governing organization, however, Baptist churches were autonomous, and local congregations decided the matter for themselves.

The earlier efforts of a group of Scotch-Irish immigrants led by Presbyterian minister David Rice paved the way for the work of the Baptist ministers. As early as 1792, when Kentucky framed its first state constitution, Reverend Rice led a group to push for excluding slavery in the state. An organization known as Friends of Humanity was formed in Kentucky in 1807. Led by eleven ministers and thirteen laymen of several denominations, the group promoted freedom for all humans.

In Tennessee, as in Kentucky, the Scotch-Irish led the way

in opposing slavery. The Manumission Society of Tennessee was established to organize abolitionists. As with the society in North Carolina, the Tennessee group collected money to purchase slave contracts in order to set the slaves free.

Leaders in East Tennessee pushed for providing education for slaves. Groups were formed in Maryville and Knoxville to spotlight the plight of the slaves and take steps to assist them. Published in Knoxville, the *Presbyterian Witness* ran an editorial that claimed there was not a solitary argument in favor of teaching a white person that could not be used in teaching a black person. The editor wrote: "If one has a soul that will never die, so has the other. If one has the suscepti-bilities of improvement, mentally, socially, and morally, so has the other. If one is bound by the laws of God to improve the talents he has received from the Creator's hands, so is the other."

It has been said through the years that the people of South-ern Appalachia are withdrawn and "hard to get to know." To a degree, this may be true. A large part of this has to do with the fact that they are very protective of their individuality and the individuality of their families. At the same time, they have always tried to assist others in acquiring the opportunity to express individuality. No place has this been better shown in Southern Appalachian history than in their support to help all creatures of God experience freedom.

The Tooth-Jumper

In 1847, Raymond Huggins gave little James Earl Morgan one of the most unusual Christmas gifts anyone has ever received. According to people who share the story, it was one of the most appreciated and most welcomed gifts of all time.

Raymond Huggins was a farmer, a preacher, and a blacksmith. Most of all, though, he was known far and wide for his skill as a first-class tooth-jumper. One of Huggins's descendants claims that Rev. Dr. Raymond Huggins was far more than a mere primitive dentist who used pain-producing pliers or pinchers to extract a tooth. His talent and expertise lay in his skillful use of a hammer and a chisel, the instruments employed by the tooth-jumpers of the era.

There were other such specialists in the Southern Highlands area, but every practitioner was not as accomplished in the art as Reverend Huggins. He was renowned for never having broken a jaw or flattened a nose or knocked out more teeth than he was supposed to. He had a steady hand, a sharp eye, and the know-how to tap the hammer on the chisel with just the right touch.

To jump a tooth, Huggins would carefully place the chisel against the ridge of the tooth giving the patient trouble. With the chisel just under the edge of the gum, Huggins would eye it cautiously, then tap it with a quick flick of the wrist. That's where people said Huggins's secret of success lay—in the smooth flick of the wrist. According to the patients Huggins treated, nine times out of ten the tooth would jump right out, and the thankful patient wouldn't feel a thing.

Now it was Christmas Eve, and little James Earl Morgan was painfully enduring the worst toothache he had ever experienced. For eleven months and thirty days, the little guy had been looking forward to Christmas, his favorite day of the year. It looked as if the toothache was going to overshadow the joy Christmas would bring.

James Earl's mother was well-known and respected for the doctoring she had done on her family and for others in need of her care, but this particular toothache was one thing she just couldn't conquer. She had tried all kinds of roots and herbs and sassafras teas, but the cure for this lowly toothache escaped her. That's why she decided to take James Earl to Eli Gibbons, a man who lived nearby who was supposed to be pretty good with a pair of pliers.

As soon as James Earl saw Old Man Gibbons pick up the awkward-looking homemade pliers, the little guy started howling. Then, when Gibbons suggested they place hot ash poultices upon the tooth to prepare it for extraction, James Earl threw a fit, jerked away from his mother's grasp, and ran all the way home. Once there, he crawled under his bed and claimed he was never coming out again.

James Earl's older brother suggested they borrow some of their mother's yarn and tie one end to the tooth and the other to a tree limb; then James Earl could climb up into the tree and jump. This method was more appealing than Gibbons's pliers, so James Earl agreed to give it a try.

Everything seemed to be working fine until he jumped. When he hit the ground, James Earl discovered that the yarn had broken and that the tooth was still in his mouth, throbbing away. Besides that, he sprained his ankle and had to go down to the river and break a hole in the ice so he could soak away the swelling.

What a Christmas! James Earl thought as he sat on the river bank and contemplated ending it all by diving through the hole in the ice and sinking to the bottom. His tooth was throbbing worse than ever, and his foot was turning bluer by the minute, when he heard his mother's excited voice come out of the woods and bounce upon the water.

"James Earl!" his mother yelled as she walked crisply up the river bank toward him. "James Earl," she declared proudly, "look who I got!"

"Who?" James Earl replied, turning to look into the face of a long lean man with a dark beard.

"The Rev. Dr. Raymond Huggins," his mother answered. She had located Huggins, who lived quite a distance from them, and had explained to him how he was the only person who could possibly relieve little James Earl of his misery on Christmas Eve.

Wasting little time and no words, Huggins quickly set about doing what he had to do. It was all over before James Earl really understood what was happening. Even the swelling in his ankle seemed to subside when the tooth jumped out. It was the most memorable Christmas he had ever experienced. And from that episode came the story James Earl told to his children and grandchildren every Christmas Eve for the rest of his life.

The Birth of Gatlinburg

The family names *Ogle* and *Huskey* are prominent in Sevier County, Tennessee. At the end of the Revolutionary War in 1783, William "Billy" Ogle married Martha Jane Huskey, who was part Cherokee. They moved from Virginia to Edgefield District, South Carolina, and then to Wilkes County, Georgia, where his name is listed on the 1785 tax roll. Then, the 1790 federal census lists Billy as head of a household in Edgefield District. Records show that he and Martha Jane purchased land there in 1795 and 1796, and the federal census again lists him in Edgefield District in 1800. Martha Jane's brother, Peter Huskey, is also on record for acquiring land in Edgefield District.

Billy Ogle liked to wander, hunt, and trade. His adventures led him to visit the Great Smoky Mountains. Because of his wife's heritage, he was given access to hunt on the land and to trade with the Eratis, a branch of the Cherokees living in the Smokies. Billy fell in love with the area. On one of his trips, he acquired some land near a stream and a waterfall. Then, he and his Eratis friends notched logs and fashioned a foundation for a cabin.

He returned to South Carolina and told his family and friends that he had located "paradise" and had laid the foundation for a cabin there. He told of plenty of hunting in the dense woodlands and ample fishing in crystal clear streams.

He told of the rich loam soil for vegetable gardens and, more importantly, how there were no mosquitoes nor danger of malaria. In South Carolina, mosquitoes were posing a big problem. Malaria had started taking lives prior to Billy's departure for the Smokies. Upon his return, he found that an epidemic had broken out. Billy's family and friends were eager to relocate in his paradise.

Before Billy could make arrangements to sell his land, however, he became extremely ill and quickly died. He was buried near Fruit Hill, in Edgefield District, South Carolina, in 1803. Martha wasted no time in gathering together her five sons and two daughters to move from the area. She had older children, already married and with families of their own, who wanted to make the trip with her.

Martha's brother Peter Huskey and his wife and younger children, along with his married children and their families, joined the exodus. First they went to Virginia to stay with relatives for a while and to make preparations for their long journey. Then, combining land and water travel, the large party overcame many challenges and eventually arrived in the area originally called White Oak Flats. They found Billy's cabin foundation and built on it. (Today, the Arrowmont School of Arts and Crafts and Pi Beta Phi's staff house surround the original cabin site. Pi Beta Phi moved the original cabin and had it reconstructed near where Baskins Creek enters the Little Pigeon River.)

In 1817, Martha and her family joined the White Oak Flats Baptist Church, which was located across the road from her property. This was a mission that had been established by the Baptist church in Sevierville. The town of Sevierville, originally called "Forks of the River," had been officially established in 1795, after veterans of the Revolutionary War had settled there.

As the 1800s progressed, White Oak Flats grew into a self-sufficient mountain community. Other families followed the

Ogles and Huskeys to settle in the Smokies. These early families, whose names are also common in the area, included the Whaley, Maples, Oakley, Bales, and Emert families. The pioneers settled in surrounding valleys and coves, in areas given such picturesque names as Greenbrier, the Sugarlands, Roaring Fork, Elkmont, the Glades, and Fighting Creek. Meanwhile, the community of White Oak Flats prospered with the influx of new families.

White Oak Flats became Gatlinburg just prior to the Civil War, and many people through the years have inquired as to how this renaming occurred.

Well, the story of the change has a couple of different twists. It is a known fact that the first general store in White Oak Flats belonged to the Ogles and was the only store for quite a few years. Then as the town continued to grow, a man by the name of Radford Gatlin moved to the area and opened a second general store. The explanation from here takes on two different endings.

One account has it that Gatlin was approached by town leaders and asked if a small post office could be set up in a corner of his store. Some say he was approached because the Ogles didn't want to fool with a post office, or because there had been bickering between the Ogles and some other citizens, or because it appeared that Gatlin might have more room for the post office. Whatever the case, this account claims that Gatlin okayed the post office, with the stipulation that all mail sent to it would be addressed to "Gatlinburg." The account contends that the leaders took him up on his proposition, and Gatlinburg had its beginning.

The second account, however, doesn't treat Radford Gatlin so kindly. It claims that most of the community folks didn't appreciate Gatlin, frowned upon his morals, and took note that he was said to have used "tainted" money to move to the area and open up his business. Supposedly, people were also displeased that Gatlin had a female slave. When tales began to circulate throughout the community that Gatlin's slave had mysteriously vanished one night and that he had killed and buried her, some of the community leaders approached him with a proposal.

It is alleged they told Gatlin that if he would agree to sell his store and post office at a fair price, move out of the community and never return, then White Oak Flats would officially change its name to Gatlinburg. Supposedly, Gatlin accepted the offer. So, it appears that Gatlinburg could possibly be the only town in existence to be named after a scoundrel simply because the folks of the community wanted to rid the area of his kind!

Note: Tennessee state records document that William Trentham was appointed the first and only postmaster of White Oak Flats in 1840. The position was discontinued in 1844. These same records show that Radford Gatlin was appointed the first postmaster of Gatlinburg in 1856. Elijah Ogle was appointed Gatlinburg postmaster in 1858, followed by the appointments of James Cardwell in 1859, Ephraim Reagan in 1866, Richard Reagan in 1871, and Ephraim Ogle in 1883. Ephraim Ogle was also appointed in 1889, with three other postmasters in between his times of service. Then, Ephraim Ogle was appointed again in 1897, with one postmaster in between. The records also state that White Oak Flats was unofficially called Gatlinburg in 1856, but did not officially become Gatlinburg until 1893.

The above information gives credence to a third, but less circulated account: Gatlin housed the post office, became postmaster, and saw the named changed to Gatlinburg. However, because he later aired his controversial political views regarding slavery and other matters, he suffered a severe beating, was ordered out of town, and told never to return.

Mahala Mullins

Mahala Mullins was born in 1824 and died in 1902, but people still talk about this woman, who was known from one end of the Southern Appalachians to the other. According to reports, everyone who knew Mahala liked her, unless they somehow made her mad. If they rubbed her the wrong way, they were in deep trouble. She was said to have always been fair, honest, and truthful, even though some of the tales surrounding her life may have been embellished.

Mahala was Melungeon, an ethnic group unique to Southern Appalachia. She was said to have shared some of the striking physical characteristics common to her ancestry: beautiful, deep-olive skin, high cheekbones, and gorgeous black or gray eyes, along with black hair.

Melungeons still exist in Tennessee, mainly in Hancock County. They are a mysterious people. Not even the descendants are sure of their ancestry. Most historians feel the question of Melungeon family lineage will never be answered. They have lived here for centuries, and even the name, *Melungeon,* is one of unknown origin. Some say it comes from a French word, *mélange,* which means *mixture.* Others, however, claim the name derives from *melungo,* an African-Portuguese term meaning *sailor.* Perhaps the latter word is the correct one, for many Melungeons believe they descend from a band of Portuguese sailors who mutinied before 1776 and settled on the coast of North Carolina. Some historians say these people could have descended from Carthaginians or Welsh Indians.

By far one of the most popular theories, however, concerns the Spanish explorer Hernando de Soto, who in 1540 traveled from Florida as far as Memphis, Tennessee, to search for gold. The story goes that some of the explorer's men became lost or were captured by the Cherokees. Supposedly, these Spaniards intermarried with the Cherokees to produce the Melungeon people. Whatever the case, the Melungeons have been the subject of many tales and much folklore.

Mahala Mullins's size was one of the main reasons the lore surrounding her grew to become larger than life. Some claim she tipped the scales at 600 pounds and stood seven and a half feet tall! Reportedly, this mountain of a woman could heft a yearling bull over her head with ease. Supposedly, when she sat down to a light meal, she commonly downed an entire pig, along with other morsels! Mahala was said to have been able to rip a firm-rooted pine from the earth with one hand. People swore they saw her splinter a two-inch oak plank with her bare fist!

The absolute facts concerning Mahala continue to be hidden. Belonging to neither the Caucasian, African, nor Cherokee world, the Melungeons kept to themselves in the deep isolation of the back hills. Friends and relatives, however, claimed that the weight attributed to Mahala has been greatly exaggerated. By their words, Mahala weighed only between 350-400 pounds. They explained that she looked larger because she developed a disease we know today as *elephantiasis*, characterized by a swelling of body parts, especially the arms and legs. They said that she was taller than the average person, but probably not seven feet or more.

Legend has it that when Mahala died, a wall from one side of her house had to be removed, and her body was wrapped in a blanket and gently rolled down the mountain. Friends and relatives said there was some truth to this, but that she was actually removed from the house through a fireplace opening. It seems that the opening had been left for a chimney when the house had been built, but Mahala died before the chimney was added. As far as being rolled down the mountain in a blanket, friends and relatives say this is not true.

Instead, according to eyewitness reports, some men sawed the legs off of the four-poster bed Mahala died on, and then they nailed planks around it to form a box. Friends and relatives then carried the bed/box/casket to a nearby cemetery.

The beautiful part of this mention of Mahala Mullins, however, is that she loved people. Her feats of strength and the stories of how she "whipped" scoundrels whom she thought were doing wrong to others are still legend. Many people claimed the biggest part of Mahala was her heart. While some adults may have feared her, all children adored her. They saw and felt the gigantic love this unique woman had to give.

The Red Berry Between Two Hills of Snow

Some of the stories in this volume are definitely true. No doubt about them. Others have been handed down without absolute historical references to support them. This, however, does not mean they are not based on truth. The account of Mary "Star" Summers began its oral tradition in the early 1800s and still survives in some niches of Appalachia.

John and Alice Summers married rather late in life. One result of this late marriage is that they had only one child, a girl they named Mary. It is said that Mary was one of the most beautiful of God's creatures. She had sparkling ebony eyes, skin like pure snow, and shiny black hair. By the time she was five years old, everyone ceased calling her Mary, replacing this with the more descriptive name of "Star."

John and Alice Summers had left the Northeast and traveled to the Southern Appalachians to find land and stake their claim. Several years after they resettled, Star was born. It was a sparsely populated area, and Star did not have many children to play with. However, there was one little boy named James Gaines who became Star's inseparable playmate.

Hours on end, the children played in the hills and along the river bank. Their favorite game was hide-and-seek. When it came Star's time to hide, James would close his eyes and appropriately say aloud, "Twinkle, twinkle, little Star, how I wonder where you are!"

Late one afternoon, when Star was seven and James was almost eight, the two children were absorbed in their favorite game, and Star was hiding. Playing near a creek that flowed into the river, they got a little deeper into the woods than usual. Because James had stopped to get rid of a pebble in his shoe, Star was given more time to hide.

As is often the case in the mountains, a sudden rainstorm approached, and the sky grew unusually dark. The downpour began quickly. James called out to Star. There was no answer. Frantically, he began to call out time and again. Fearing that Star had been swept away by the sudden rising creek, James ran back to the cabins for help.

Star's parents and neighbors searched for her all night with no success. For days, with little rest, the hunt continued. There was never even a trace of Star. Her parents' grief was heavy. For a time, her mother stayed in bed, depressed, not wanting to speak with anyone. Her father continued to work.

Years dragged by. Everyone but Alice Summers gave up any hope of ever finding Star. Most believed that she had been, indeed, swept away by the raging water that tragic evening. Though he never mentioned it to his wife, John Summers agreed with the neighbors. As James Gaines grew into a fine-looking young man, he wanted to side with Mrs. Summers. His heart was still with Star. In his mind, however, he had to agree with the others.

James remained close to the Summers. Star's parents aged faster than they should have, so James was faithful in helping them in any way he could. After working for his own family, he would daily go to the Summers' house to assist them. Alice appreciated James and began to feel as if he were her son. He helped to fill the void left by the loss of Star.

Alice also appreciated a rugged old fur trader named McGregor. He traveled the mountains, never knowing an

enemy, passing freely among both the whites and the Cherokees. People loved McGregor and trusted him. Each spring
and fall he would come by the Summers' place and spend a
few days with them. The stories he told and the bagpipes he
played lifted the spirits of all who came in contact with him.
Alice especially looked forward to his visits and the inspiration he brought.

When McGregor first learned of the family's misfortune, he
kept his eyes and ears open for any sign of Star. Finally, after
several years, he told John, "I know Alice thinks Star is still
alive. Were she alive, however, I would have seen her or heard
of her existence during my travels."

One spring, McGregor did not show. Alice was greatly disappointed. Fall came and went, but still no McGregor. This
caused Alice to take a turn for the worse, because she lived for
the day when McGregor would come, along with his funny
stories and bagpipes, and share the news that Star was alive.

McGregor reappeared the spring that James Gaines was
due to reach his seventeenth birthday. James, John, and Alice
gathered together to hear the latest news from McGregor. The
old fur trader passed along some stories, most of them
humorous, and played his bagpipes with as much zest as ever.
Then, he told them that he had a message to deliver to all the
families who lived near the banks of the river.

"In my travels," he said, "I have often bypassed the cabin
of old Chief Skenondah. He would never trade with me
because he does not like any white man. He has slain many
of our people. I have always considered it a compliment that
he would allow me to pass through his land unharmed. This
year, however, as I entered his area, he sought me out. He told
me that there is a family in this part of the country who will
understand his message."

Alice and John exchanged glances. James looked at both of
them. "What is the message?" Alice asked hopefully.

"The old chief said I was to announce, 'There exists two

hills of snow, between which grows a berry, as red as the setting sun. The family who comes to claim this treasure shall have it.'"

Alice sprang from her chair. She looked wildly at McGregor, then collapsed like a rag doll. James grabbed her to keep her from hitting the split-pine floor. The other two men assisted him as he placed Alice in her bed. They worked with wet cloths to help her regain consciousness.

As Alice opened her eyes, she said, "Star is alive. She is alive and we must claim her!"

"But, Alice—" John began.

"No time to talk!" his wife interrupted. "We must leave at once!"

Wide-eyed, James said, "Mrs. Summers, are you sure—"

She didn't give him a chance to finish. All three men had to restrain her as she fought to go after Star immediately.

"I'll go, Alice," John Summers assured her as the three of them led her to bed again. Her face, which had been as white as the bedsheets, was now flushed. "First light, I'll go," John reassured her.

"Let me go, Mr. Summers," James insisted.

Before John could argue, McGregor broke in. "Yes, let James go," he said. "The trail is long and rough. He, with youth on his side and traveling alone, will have a better chance of getting there swiftly." They no longer questioned Alice. Her voice, facial expressions, and actions told them they must discover the truth.

That evening, James made ready for what would be a rough ordeal. McGregor drew a map and gave him detailed instructions for the trip. At daybreak, James checked his supplies, mounted his horse, and was on his way. For three days, he carefully looked out for Cherokees and wild animals as he struggled to follow the directions supplied by McGregor. He traveled from sunup to sundown, not wasting one ray of light. Each short evening, he camped under the stars, whispering

36

the poem from childhood: "Twinkle, twinkle, little Star, how I wonder where you are!"

On the afternoon of the fourth day, James came to a landmark McGregor had described to him. A creek branched out to form a "Y." At the fork of the Y was a once-majestic oak tree, now dead, having been struck by lightning. Behind that tree was a healthy one, taller than any oak James had ever seen. From the tree's branches hung dozens of scalps—trophies as well as warning signs, collected by the old chief and his people. James knew he was entering the land of Skenondah.

The forest beyond the Y was dense. Leading his horse, James had to cut a trail as he went. He carefully marked his path in order to find his way out again. As night fell, he was more afraid than he had ever been in his life. Some animals wailed, while owls and other night birds screeched, upset with his intrusion into their territory. This was one evening that he dare not sleep.

As dawn broke, James came to a clearing and one of the most beautiful lakes he had ever seen. It was even more beautiful than McGregor had described it. Several cabins circled the lake. James quickly located the largest cabin, mounted his horse, and rode toward it.

As James approached the dwelling, he saw a freshly dug grave. He had observed Cherokee graves before. By the markers on this one, he knew it was the final resting place of a young maiden. His hopes crashed. The exhaustion James had been fighting now leapt up to grab him and pull him down. He stumbled over to the grave and fell upon the damp dirt. Sobbing, he went to sleep.

James did not know how many hours he had slept before he was awakened by a piercing stare. It was the type of quiet presence that is louder than noise. The young man opened his eyes, rubbed them, then turned to look at the most wrinkled face he had ever seen. It was an old Cherokee with an unbelievable number of creases etched into his leathery skin.

The man looked as if he had just returned from a ceremonial ritual. James arose and started to address this person, who he knew must be Chief Skenondah. The old Cherokee spoke first.

"You look like a whipped animal," he said in a deep, resonant voice, speaking English as if it were his own language.

James stuttered, "I . . . I have come to claim the red berry between two hills of snow." His eyes dropped toward the grave he had been sleeping on. Chief Skenondah pointed toward the grave, palm upward, and said, sadly, "This is my own daughter, Half Moon. Shooting Star was a sister to her. Is it Shooting Star you wish to claim?"

As McGregor had instructed, James spoke only the words he had been given. "I have come to claim the red berry between two hills of snow." The old chief stepped into the forest and returned shortly with a young lady who had sparkling ebony eyes and smooth white skin. Her shiny black hair was combed back from her forehead, lying across her shoulders in two long braids. James knew immediately that this lovely maiden was Star.

With his knife, Chief Skenondah reached over and carefully cut the girl's buckskin blouse, revealing a portion of her snow-white breasts. Between them was a small round birthmark, as red as a berry. The chief led her by the hand toward James, signaled for him to extend his hand, then placed her hand in his.

Skenondah spoke. "I promised my daughter that Shooting Star would now go to her own people. Take her. I go to the setting sun." With these words, the elderly Cherokee leader turned and walked away. Tears ran from Star's eyes, but she stayed with James as he placed his arm around her.

Chief Skenondah—the man who had been a father to Star for the past ten years—now lifted two heavy, stone-filled bags. With difficulty, he carried them to a canoe docked at the lake. After lifting several large stones into the canoe, he attached the stone-filled bags to himself, stepped into the

38

canoe, and pushed away from the shore.

While Star and James watched, the old man paddled toward the center of the lake. Singing his death song, he stroked toward the deepest part of the water. He then lifted his tomahawk and brought it down sharply, splintering the bottom of the canoe. Star turned toward James, burying her face into his shoulder as the boat began to sink. Soon, only two white paddles floated on the glistening water.

Old Christmas

Miss Maggie, an elderly lady of the mountains, told me about Old Christmas. According to her, many mountain people used to celebrate Christmas in January. "My grandfather always celebrated Christmas on January 6," she informed me. "He refused to acknowledge December 25 as the real Christmas, claiming it was man-made." I asked Miss Maggie if there was any difference between the way Old Christmas was celebrated and the way we celebrate contemporary Christmas.

"Oh, yes," she said. Then she went on to tell me that in many ways the two were just the opposite in the methods of celebration. According to her, Old Christmas was much more subdued than is our modern holiday. Rather than having an abundance of loud music, merrymaking, and excitement, Old Christmas was celebrated with prayer and soft a cappella singing. It was a quiet, reflective time. Folks put away their fiddles and banjos as they assumed a calm, prayerful attitude.

Miss Maggie said, "Grandfather used to tell me how they gathered around the fireplace when he was a boy and sang the Cherry Tree Carol, which told of the birth of Christ." She shared some of the words of the carol with me:

On the sixth day of January
His birthday shall be,
When the stars and the mountains

Shall tremble with glee.
As Joseph was a-walking,
Thus did the angels sing;
And Mary's son at midnight
Was born to be our king.

Interested in what the elderly lady told me, I researched the subject to learn more about the origin and the specific reason for the January 6 observance. That's when I learned how the twelve days of Christmas were once celebrated in the mountains, beginning on December 25 and ending on the evening of January 5. This custom was inherited by the mountain people from their European ancestors. Down through the years, many people began to discard the twelve-day celebration while retaining the January 6 observance for Christmas.

Like Miss Maggie's grandfather claimed, the January 6 observance was subdued, following twelve festive days. Beginning on December 25 and continuing until the evening of January 5, there was much excitement, an abundance of merrymaking, banjo picking, quilting bees, dances, and all sorts of goings-on by the mountain people. This is when they would sing the song their European ancestors once sang:

On the twelfth day of Christmas, my true love sent to me
Twelve drummers drumming,
Eleven pipers piping,
Ten lords a-leaping,
Nine ladies dancing,
Eight maids a-milking,
Seven swans a-swimming,
Six geese a-laying,
Five golden rings.
Four colly birds,
Three French hens,
Two turtle doves
And a partridge in a pear tree.

On Old Christmas Eve, the twelve days of celebrating came to an end, and the holiday took on a different light. The loud singing ceased and the dancing stopped as the frivolous air was pushed aside. Before midnight, the family would sit around the hearth and listen to the eldest member tell of the birth of Christ. Other members would talk about the promise of peace and brotherhood that came with that birth.

Old Christmas Eve was called the Night of Miracles. The older members of the family instructed the children to quietly walk to the barn. There, they supposedly could see their animals humbly kneel in observance of Christ's birth. Some of the older folks even claimed that the animals would speak and that water would turn to wine, evidence that miracles were still happening.

Finally, as the clock hands crept past midnight and Old Christmas arrived, it was customary to bring out a jug of sweet cider and sing: "Love and joy come to you / And to you your wassail too / And God bless you and send you a happy New Year / And God send you a happy New Year."

They would then burn a piece of cedar or some type of fir in the fireplace. As they sat quietly and looked at the flames, they would reflect inwardly, praising God for the birth of Christ and for the blessings of His birth.

From Enemies to Friends

"Grandma was a wife and mother at sixteen," Naomi Chapman said. "She lived on the outskirts of the Smokies on the North Carolina side of the Little Pigeon River. A tribe of Cherokees had escaped to this area when the government moved their people west in 1838. This tribe set up camp on the other bank of the river, and when the water froze, they came asking for food. Food was not too plentiful among the settlers, and they hated to part with it."

Naomi went on to tell how her grandfather had stored some turnips in the cellar, but the smell had grown so strong that he decided to give the turnips to the Cherokees. One morning, Naomi's grandmother, still a young woman at the time, was baking bread when three Cherokees, two women and a man, just opened the door and walked in. According to Naomi, they never knocked. Naomi's grandmother was proud of the pine floor in her kitchen and always kept it immaculate. That day, the visitors tracked in mud and stood there with water dripping onto the clean floor.

Naomi's grandmother gave them the turnips, but still they stayed. "Grandma knew they smelled the bread baking," Naomi said. "She left it in the oven as long as she could, but finally had to take it out or it would burn. She thought she would probably have to give them one loaf. As she placed the pans on the back of the stove after turning the fresh loaves out on the kitchen table, out of the corner of her eye she saw each woman take a loaf and put it under her blanket."

Then, according to Naomi, the man reached for the last loaf, and that's when the young homemaker exploded. She grabbed her rolling pin and cracked him sharply across the knuckles. He let out a howl, dropped the bread, and bounded through the door, quickly catching up with the two women, who had already departed after getting their loaves. Angry, his pride damaged, the man slapped one of the women and took her loaf away. Naomi's grandmother watched the three of them go down the road tearing big chunks out of her bread and eating it.

When Naomi's grandfather came home, her grandmother told him of the experience. He was frightened and told her never to hit a Cherokee, regardless of how rude they might be. He said there was no telling what they might do for reprisal. "After all," he said, "the government did make them move, and they'll never get over that." Naomi's grandfather began to keep a close watch for Cherokees and told the rest of the family to do the same.

It wasn't long after that, however, that the tables turned. This time it was Naomi's grandfather who became directly involved. He worked in a general store where they sold just about everything—traps, sugar, kerosene, piece goods. One day, a Cherokee woman came to the store when Naomi's grandfather was by himself. Before entering, the woman removed her papoose from her back and placed the baby outside the door. A hungry boar came along, sniffed the animal skin covering the baby, and decided it would make a good meal. The boar rooted the baby over and pitched in with tusks and hooves, luckily beginning at the baby's feet.

The baby screamed, and Naomi's grandfather ran out to the scene. With heavy boots and a broom, he fought off the hungry animal and rescued the papoose. Cherokees appeared like magic to see what was going on. When they finally understood what had happened, they agreed with the mother that she should give the papoose to Naomi's grandfather. It was with extreme difficulty that he finally convinced the woman that he could not accept her gift. He explained that he had nothing against her custom, but that it just wasn't the way his people did things.

The Cherokee mother still insisted that Naomi's grandfather be paid. So to show her gratitude, she instructed her husband to paint a sign and place it over the door of the family's home. Naomi said, "I can't recall exactly what my mother told me the sign read, but no more Cherokees came around begging for food. As a matter of fact, Grandma would often be out of the kitchen and come back in to find berries, grain, and sometimes even a squirrel or some other type of game upon the kitchen table."

Out of the Darkness

Shortly after the Revolutionary War, a pioneer named Burns wandered into southeastern Kentucky, liked what he found, and stayed. He married, reared a family, and laid the foundation for his clan. Years passed, and Burns's great-grandson became a mountain minister, cast in the mold of early Calvinism and ordained into the Baptist denomination. Everyone called him Preacher Burns, and the people in the area where he lived had developed an extremely clan-oriented mentality. Family ties were strong; feuds between families were frequent, bitter, and long lasting.

Feelings between the Burns and Combs clans were especially bad. In this atmosphere, Preacher Burns ranged up and down the mountains, proclaiming the Christian gospel and stressing the need for a universal, unconditional love. The people listened to Preacher Burns, but they filtered his message. What he said proved to have little effect upon the feuding. So, in the mid-1800s, the minister moved to Virginia.

Virginia was much like his own southeastern Kentucky, but was not ravaged by bloody quarrels between families. Here, Preacher Burns thought, he could rear his own family without fear that his sons and daughters would become involved in the feuds.

James Burns, the minister's youngest son, was born in Virginia. Raised in the mountains and the forests, James developed into a strong, sturdy young man with keen insights and senses. Little formal education was afforded him, though— he had spent only ten months in school. James's father did teach him the biblical principles as best he could.

When James was twenty-one, his father died, and the young man soon returned to the home of his clan, in Clay County, Kentucky. There, he found what his father had fled from many years before. The whole area was still aflame with feuding. Many of his relatives had been killed, and the supreme purpose in the lives of those remaining was to avenge their kin.

James Burns's strength, accurate shooting eyes, and courage made him a welcome sight. One evening, not long after his arrival, James led an attack upon enemies of his family, where he was wounded and left for dead. The next morning, however, he found himself resting in a home of the rivals. He was near death, but the "enemies" nursed him back to health and eventually sent him on his way. Arriving home, James went into the woods to reflect upon what had happened. For what purpose, he asked himself, had he been spared? Why was he now alive and well when both families in the feuding had considered him dead?

After much soul-searching, James recalled his father's teachings and came to grips with the present. He now believed that God had singled him out to lead his people out of the darkness of hate. Through God's power he had to help them overcome a condition that began generations ago. God seemed to open a curtain and reveal to him that the people were still caught in the clutches of a feud mentality that went all the way back to Scotland, when families had to band together in clans for protection and survival. James's challenge was to help them open up the shut-in view. Through God's leadership, he knew he must take on the task of erasing the senseless feuding that seemed to be the curse of the isolated mountains.

James knew that the mountain people were not consciously troublemakers. They really desired peace, but peace had been sacrificed for misplaced honor and misplaced duty. In order to help them, however, James felt he must withdraw from them for a period of preparation. He sought additional formal education and received it in a little Baptist college in Ohio.

In 1892, James returned again to Clay County. He was twenty-seven years old and had come back to help his people broaden their vision. He began by establishing a quality education program. As he instructed students, he continued to study, jumping at every opportunity to improve his own education. When he wasn't teaching school, he was attending school. He was away at Berea College in 1898-1899, where he decided he must start a college in the heart of his own land.

With no money but much faith, James returned to Clay County once again to present his new idea. He introduced this idea to the family leaders gathered in an old mill, the largest meeting room in the area. The air was tense, but James pulled no punches. He told them that the time had come for a new era in the mountains.

"There is a higher call for people created in the image of God," James proclaimed. "Your children should be messengers of heaven instead of agents of hell!"

Many years later, James said, "Except for me, that was a very quiet meeting. I didn't know what they were going to do. But I was right glad when Lee Combs got up, and when Dan Burns got up, and they met in front of me. They didn't draw their guns, but they shook hands. Then I knew that Oneida College was going to be a success."

Early Conflicts

In the early 1800s, when industry was growing in the eastern part of America, the residents in and around the Smoky Mountains were still mostly an agricultural people. There were no large towns in the area, and very few villages existed. Jonesborough was the largest settlement, containing less than a hundred log cabins.

In the late 1700s and early 1800s, Knoxville was little more than a farming hamlet. It was the hub of an agricultural district with a radius of about fifteen miles and a total population of approximately 500 people. Some of these Knoxville residents, like John Sevier, for example, lived in homes on their plantations but also kept a town residence, because of official duties or because it brought them more contact with the outside world.

Both the town houses and the country homes during this time were simple and rustic. A traveler could not journey a mile in any direction along the valley of any of the waterways without coming upon a few cleared acres, enclosed within a brush fence. In the middle of the clearing would be a one-story cabin of unhewn logs. About twenty square feet in size, the cabin would be roofed with split poplar and have an exterior oversized chimney of sticks and clay. The windows would be covered with coarse paper, made transparent by a smearing of bear's grease. At night, the windows would be protected by heavy, stoutly barred shutters, which, along with strong doors, helped keep out intruders.

Above the cabin's doorway, there was a narrow opening that served as a lookout and a porthole in case of attack. No one ever opened the door in the morning until looking through the opening to make sure no enemy was lurking around the cabin. The settlers usually kept the area around the cabin free of bushes and trees, not wanting their enemies to use such things for cover.

The enemies at this time were the Cherokees. The conflict had become almost unresolvable earlier, when the Cherokees signed a treaty that bound them to fight alongside the British during the Revolutionary War. Because of the animosity between the settlers and the Cherokees, constant precautions had to be observed.

One lady told me of how her great-grandmother had to stand guard over her father and brothers as they worked in the fields. Wielding a rifle, she would perch herself upon the roof of their little cabin or on a hill overlooking the clearing. Constantly surveying in all directions, she would keep the rifle cocked while the men tended the crops.

There was at least one time when my informant's great-grandmother fired at some intruders. Her father and brothers then picked up their rifles, and a battle ensued. In the end, two of the Cherokees were left for dead, and the others scattered. The men resumed their plowing, and the lookout reloaded her gun.

Another story from this same time period is still remembered by some elderly East Tennesseans who heard it from their parents and grandparents. It concerns Major James Cozby and relates how he outwitted a band of angry Cherokees who had surrounded his house after nightfall. Major Cozby's animals were making noises of unrest, warning him that prowlers were sneaking up on the cabin. Major Cozby peeked through his porthole and spied a band of about twenty attackers quietly approaching his home.

No one was in the house with Cozby except for his wife and their four small children. Cozby quickly barricaded the door, extinguished the flame in the fireplace and primed his two rifles. With his wife at the back-door porthole and himself at the front, he spent the night giving orders in a loud, confident voice to his platoon—a platoon comprised of the four small children.

The Major's ruse succeeded. The intruders were held at bay as they listened to the powerful commands and strategy coming from within the dark cabin. With the first streak of dawn, the would-be marauders silently filtered away into the forest.

Mountaineer Creativity

According to Vertie Sharp, her parents were married in the late 1800s and settled in the Great Smoky Mountains area. Vertie's first memories are of a little log cabin in which she and her family lived by a small stream.

"We had a sod fireplace and a little stove for cooking," Vertie told me. "Along with the wood, our family burned cobs, cornstalks, and cow chips in both the fireplace and the stove." Vertie recalled how her father made a table and other furniture that was very sturdy but, in her words, "not very polished." At the table, her mother and father would sit on a couple of kegs, while the children stood to eat.

"Our parents didn't even have a table when they were first married," Vertie said. "They sat on logs and ate the food spread out on the bed. When I was about nine, a man came by our house and wanted to get a keg of pickles. He traded my daddy a chair for the pickles, and everyone in the area came by our house to see the newfangled piece of furniture."

The first school Vertie ever attended was in a neighbor's two-room house. Since all the other cabins in the area had only one room, his place was selected for the school. The children had to furnish their own books, so very seldom did any of the students have books alike. They also brought their own seats to school, if they had any seats to bring. No desks were available, but the school did furnish a long wooden table on which they could work. Vertie's first teacher was a seventeen-year-old boy who was paid $12.00 per month for his efforts.

Living a long distance from the nearest doctor/dentist, Vertie and her family often had to postpone going for medical treatment as long as possible. According to Vertie, "Mama had a toothache for several months during the winter when she was pregnant, and there was no relief until spring. She had to wait until her baby was born and a month old, then we made the long trip to the doctor."

Speaking of babies, Vertie recalled how the women used to take care of their babies while still doing all the work around the house. "Mothers would sometimes place their larger babies in one end of the cradle and the smaller babies in the other end. As the larger baby played, it would juggle the cradle and keep the smaller baby content.

"Mama used to put my little sister in a high chair that daddy built. She would put molasses on the baby's fingers and tie a feather to the baby's wrist. That kept my little sister entertained and happy for hours on end.

"One woman often put her baby in the cradle and gave him a piece of fat meat to suck on. She tied a string to the meat and attached the other end of the string to the baby's big toe. That way, if the baby choked on the meat, he would start kicking and pull the meat out."

Vertie's mother always made Christmas gifts for all her children. Vertie said, "One of my most treasured gifts was a matchbox covered with pretty paper and decorated with pictures from a seed catalog. Another favorite was a cardboard star covered with tinfoil from a tea package that came from England.

"Daddy liked to make things for us, too. From the remains of one of Mama's broken-down washboards, he made very nice little washboards for all of us girls. With an old cultivator, he made my brother the nicest snow sled in the entire area."

Some of Vertie's fondest memories pertained to the traveling shoemaker and the stories he would tell. The whole family looked forward to his arrival every winter, and they would always have animal hides tanned and ready for him to make into shoes. Often staying several weeks, he made shoes for every member of the family.

The children were always proud of their new shoes, but they were even more interested in the adventure stories and the news of other people and places that the shoemaker brought with him.

The Visit

It was getting close to Christmas 1886 as the Reverend Zelo Harper and his wife, Elizabeth, sat in the comfort of their cabin and warmed themselves by the fireplace. Eight inches of freshly fallen snow framed their cabin in the Smoky Mountains, but finally the flurries had lost their intensity, and it looked like the storm was about to end.

"I better go now," the minister told his wife as he looked out the cabin's only window. He had already planned to visit a sick parishioner as soon as the snow let up. Elizabeth, accustomed to the seriousness with which her husband stuck to his duties, didn't try to persuade him not to go. Instead, she simply informed him that she would make the trip with him.

"Wrap up," he replied to her announcement, "and bring the bearskin robe." He didn't attempt to talk her out of accompanying him. He knew she was just as stubborn as he was. The minister went to the barn to hitch their horse to the sled. Elizabeth laid down the sweater she had been knitting, put another hickory log on the fire, adjusted the damper to let it burn as slowly as possible, then wrapped the sadirons in some burlap to put at their feet as they rode in the sled.

The sun hadn't been down long when they started on their trip of about three miles. The powdery snow muffled the sound of the horse's steady trot. The ice-laden trees, softly swaying in the wind, rang like fine crystal. The quiet beauty of the evening was suddenly disturbed, however, as the left runner of the sleigh slid into a deep rut in the road, tipping the sled at a precarious angle.

Zelo unscrambled himself from the warmth of the bearskin and sadirons, then jumped from the sled to inspect the damage. The runner was bent inward. The reverend and his wife discussed the situation, both agreeing it would be easier and safer to continue on rather than to try to turn back. Of course, they both knew that Zelo Harper wasn't much on turning back once he had started something.

Zelo walked and led the struggling horse as Elizabeth remained on the sled. He assured her it was only a short distance to the little stream that ran by the cabin of the family they were to visit. In the growing darkness, however, Zelo missed the crossing over the ice-stilled stream. For more than an hour he continued to lead the horse along the tree-lined bank as he searched for the crossing.

The wind, which had blown softly earlier, now began to pick up. Gusts of snow made the search for the crossing increasingly more difficult. Finally, weary from battling the weather, Zelo unhitched the horse and tied him to a tree. He and Elizabeth sought shelter from the icy wind near the bed of the creek.

The moon, which earlier had seemed to dissolve into the darkness, again became visible from behind scurrying clouds. This gave Zelo renewed hope, and he turned to fetch the horse to put him back in harness, but the horse was gone. Frightened by the wind and whirling snow, he had jerked on the reins, pulled himself free, and started out on his own to find shelter.

With nothing else they could do, Zelo and Elizabeth wrapped themselves in the bearskin and set out on foot to find the cabin. They appeared to be hopelessly lost. It was around 4:00 A.M. when Elizabeth fell exhausted into the snow.

"Just let me rest," she cried softly when Zelo urged her on.

"Please, just let me rest." Zelo pulled her to her feet. He realized the seriousness of the situation, knowing full well that if she should fall asleep, she would never awaken.

"No," Zelo replied to her request. He shook her roughly. "You must keep moving," he commanded. Painfully, they pressed on through the snow and ice. A few hours later, the first faint streaks of dawn tinged the dark sky, and Zelo finally consented to a moment of rest. Pausing, falling to their knees, they huddled in the robe and desperately fought the temptation to drift off into sleep.

Then, with a start, Zelo aroused from the dangerous drowsiness that had overcome him. Across the creek he thought he saw a dark object. Excitedly, he shook Elizabeth back to unwilling consciousness, and they struggled to their feet. Praying for strength, they reached down within to find the energy for what appeared to be a final effort to live.

They headed for the creek, the once-powdered snow now brittle, crunching beneath their feet. Carefully testing each stiff step, they crossed the frozen surface of the stream and sought the dark object. It was a haystack with cattle nearby.

Dawn came quickly, and with it came the sight of a path leading to the cabin they had set out to find fourteen hours earlier. The family was up and had a fire roaring in the fireplace. They answered Zelo's rap on the door, surprised to receive a visit from their pastor and his wife so early in the morning!

War of the Roses

Tennessee's gubernatorial candidates in 1886 were brothers Robert and Alfred Taylor. Bob, the Democrat, always wore a white rose in his lapel, while Alf, the Republican, displayed a red rose as his banner, earning the election race the nickname "War of the Roses." The race was the epitome of folksy Southern politics as the brothers, born and reared in the East Tennessee hamlet of Happy Valley, traveled together on the campaign trail. To save money, they even shared the same hotel room and bed as they toured the state.

The campaign was in many ways a replay of earlier days in the lives of these brothers. While they were growing up on a mountain farm, the boys argued almost daily over some public question. Neighbors would break away from their chores and come from miles around to listen to the young Democrat and young Republican "go at it" with one another.

After finishing college at Athens, Tennessee, Alf and Bob entered politics. They remained politicians the rest of their lives. Both were talented speakers, had a flair for the dramatic, were exceptional storytellers, and exhibited rare humor.

While still in school, the brothers wrote, directed, produced, and starred in a comedy to raise money for the methodist churches in the area. Entitled *Horatio Spriggins of the Firm of Muggins, Spriggins, and Scruggins,* the play gave evidence of the type of humor that would later flavor their political campaigns. The play was termed "hilarious," and a sample from it follows:

A mountaineer is on the witness stand in a murder trial.

"Tell the jury what you know about the murder on Hell Creek," says the district attorney.

"I don't know much about it," replies the witness.

"Then tell what you do know."

"All I know is this," drawls the witness. "We was all up thar at the big dance celebratin' Robert E. Lee's birthday. The fiddles was playin' and we was swingin' corners, and the boys got to slappin' each other on the back as they swung.

"Finally, one of them slapped too hard, and the other knocked him down. His brother shot that feller, and that feller's brother cut t'other feller's throat, and that feller that was knocked down drawed his knife and cut that feller's liver out. Then the old man of the house got mad and run to the bed, turned up the mattress, grabbed his shotgun, and turned both barrels loose on the crowd. I saw there was goin' to be trouble, and I left."

Bob was elected governor. He went on to attain the distinction of being governor for three terms, congressman once, then senator. Alf was later elected governor, also. He, too, became a congressman.

The brothers were astute politicians, but Tennesseans who have heard firsthand accounts about them like to recall their humorous stories, especially Bob Taylor's most famous story. The tale was so popular it became a regular feature on the lecture tours he made.

The story is about Brother Bill Patterson, a new minister in a Smoky Mountain community. In his very first sermon, he flatly condemned the devil, sin, whiskey, and all kinds of evil a body might could get into. He especially condemned, by name, one Bert Lynch. He said Lynch was a moral coward and a brute. This infuriated the bully Lynch, and he determined to give Brother Patterson a sound thrashing the next time they met. In a few days they came face-to-face on a mountain trail.

"Parson," Lynch said grimly, "you had yore turn last Sunday; it's mine today. Pull off that broadcloth and take yore medicine. I'm a-goin' to suck the marrow out'n them old bones o' yourn."

Brother Patterson pleaded with the bully, but to no avail. Finally, he said, "Well, if nothing but a fight will do you, will you let me kneel down and say my prayer before we fight?"

"All right," Lynch snapped, "but make it short."

Brother Patterson knelt down and prayed. "Lord, Thou knowest when I killed Bill Cummings and John Brown and Gerald Smith and Levi Bottles, that I did it in self-defense. Thou knowest, O Lord, that when I cut the heart out of young Michael Slinger and strewed the ground with the brains of Paddy Miles, that it was forced upon me, and that I did it with great agony of soul.

"And now, O Lord, I am about to be forced to put in his coffin this poor, miserable wretch who has attacked me here today. O Lord, have mercy upon his soul and take care of his helpless widow and orphans when he is gone."

When Brother Patterson arose, whetting the blade of his knife on the sole of his shoe, Bert Lynch was gone, leaving nothing in sight but a little cloud of dust far up the road.

The Battle of Gatlinburg

The Civil War was a terrible time for all of our nation, but maybe the worst of its consequences happened in the Southern Appalachians. Here, an unusual situation existed. A wife's family might fight against her husband's family, and, in some cases, brothers joined opposing forces.

Even though they had traveled various routes through various states, most all of the families in the Smoky Mountains and surrounding area had initially come from Virginia, a slavery stronghold. However, very few of the Southern highlanders owned slaves. The ones who sided with the Confederacy did so mainly because of honor and duty. Many of the few slaves in the area were owned by Cherokees, and when the Cherokees sided with the Confederacy, it increased the conflict between these Native Americans and the mountaineers who sided with the Union.

On June 24, 1861, Governor Isham Harris declared from the distant capital in Nashville that the entire state of Tennessee would fly the Confederate flag. This action pleased the slave owners and states' rights advocates of West and Middle Tennessee, but it divided families in East Tennessee. The majority of the mountaineers chose to disobey the order. As a result, they either joined the Union forces or fled farther up into the mountains.

Many East Tennesseans embraced Abraham Lincoln and

believed in what he wanted to accomplish. As a matter of fact, one story has it that Lincoln was actually born on the North Carolina side of the Smokies, rather than in the backwoods of Kentucky. It is said that following his birth near Mingus Creek, just north of Waynesville, his family moved to Kentucky.

Whatever the cause, numerous East Tennesseans refused to join the Confederacy. Instead, to support the Union, they gathered weapons and formed units to protest the secession. Governor Harris sent troops from Nashville, and the rebellion was stopped. A number of Union sympathizers were taken prisoner. Those found guilty of burning bridges to keep the Confederacy from gaining control of the railroad system were hanged. Others fled higher into the mountains.

It wasn't long, however, before Northern troops invaded Tennessee and crushed the Confederate opposition. The Union's General Philip Sheridan settled his men in Sevierville for the winter of 1863. Here, gristmills were set up to grind wheat and corn for the Union soldiers.

Meanwhile, in Gatlinburg, thirteen miles from Sevierville, a Confederate force of approximately 150 Cherokees and 50 white men had built a makeshift fort on a hill overlooking the town. Under the direction of Colonel William Thomas, the soldiers were mining in Alum Cave for saltpeter, to be made into gunpowder for the Confederate troops in Georgia.

Colonel William Palmer of the Union Army received orders to destroy the Confederate faction in Gatlinburg. Just before sunrise on December 11, 1863, he and his men left Sevierville on horseback and on foot. After negotiating the rough mountain trails, they arrived in Gatlinburg. Following a brief battle, the Cherokees retreated into the mountains and headed back toward their homeland in North Carolina. The remaining Confederates disbanded and scattered into the surrounding hills. The Union soldiers destroyed the fort and returned stolen livestock to their local owners.

The Battle of Gatlinburg does not stand out as a major skirmish during the Civil War. Most Civil War historians give little mention to the conflict. According to some historians, however, it is significant. They claim that even though the Cherokees and other tribesmen continued to fight in the Civil War as members of the Union or Confederacy, the Battle of Gatlinburg marked the last battle specifically between Native Americans and white men in the Eastern United States.

The Reader

A myth was born and perpetuated that pictured all mountaineers as being short on brains, long on brawn, and generally lazy. Some details from the life of Charles Cansler help to destroy such a myth.

Cansler was born in East Tennessee within a decade after the Civil War. He became a schoolteacher, worked his way up to a principal's position, and eventually became a superintendent of schools in a large city. It was after he became superintendent that he began to readily share with children and their parents some of the recollections of his own childhood.

He told of how nearly every child in his area had a little wagon and sled, usually that they had made themselves. He admitted that he was never very adept at making things, but he was able to make his own sled while his father, a woodworker and cabinetmaker, always saw to it that the children in his large family had wagons.

Charles claimed that he inherited from his mother a love for reading. He recalled how he often discovered his mother sitting up all night reading a book, after she had worked all day. Her tastes were for Dickens, Scott, Eliot, Thackeray, and other writers of the Victorian period.

Charles was especially fond of Dickens and Scott. By the time he was sixteen, he had read all of Sir Walter Scott's Waverly novels and many of the novels of Dickens. He became so interested in one of the stories that he literally couldn't put it down. Anxious about the fate of Little Nell as he read *The Old Curiosity Shop*, he hid the book in their stable's loft and would steal away to the hiding place to read, when he should have been cutting wood or performing some other task his father had given him.

"How bitterly I wept," Charles recalled in 1939, reflecting upon his childhood reading of *The Old Curiosity Shop*, "and how heavy my heart was when Little Nell died! To me, she was a real person, as were all of the characters in the books I read. I focused my mind so completely upon my reading that at times the other children of the family would be compelled to shake me if they wanted to get my attention."

Charles described himself as being a big-eyed boy with a large head and a frail, slender body. He said his mother always claimed that he had ears large enough to hear everything that was said anywhere near him, when he wasn't reading.

When Charles visited his father's shop after chores or after school, little passed among the men that he did not absorb. He was interested in one ninety-year-old man in particular. The white-haired man came by the shop at least twice a week. He was "different-looking," according to Charles's recollection, and he was full of unusual stories. Charles and his younger brother, Rex, used to stand outside the shop door and peer around at the old man curiously. They were especially interested in his "fallover" trousers that buttoned from the side, rather than from the front.

On one occasion, the old man told stories about his youthful friendship with Sam Houston, one of Charles's heroes. The man said that he had entered in an agreement with Houston to enlist under General Andrew Jackson to fight the Native Americans who were giving serious trouble to the residents of Alabama. When the enlisting officer came and Houston stepped forward to enlist, his pal changed his mind at the last moment, and Houston went alone. Houston fought heroically in the Alabama battle at Horseshoe Bend, was wounded, and attracted the attention of Andrew Jackson. The two became friends, and it was through the influence of this friendship that Houston was able to write his name indelibly upon the pages of American history.

This story stuck with Charles. Fifty years after hearing it in his father's shop, Charles wrote about it, and the story appeared in daily newspapers all over the nation. A granddaughter of the old man saw the story, and she drove many miles to visit with Charles, so she could hear the story firsthand. The granddaughter had been just a small girl when her grandfather died, and she had an indistinct recollection of him. She asked Charles many questions about her grandfather, but the most Charles remembered about him was those "fallover" breeches that buttoned from the side rather than from the front.

Charles Cansler's success story is only one of many regarding East Tennesseans who "made something of themselves." His story became an inspiration to many, because as a person of color, Charles was part of the minority in East Tennessee.

The Christmas Bells

I had never heard this story before, though the storyteller, an elderly lady born and reared in the Southern Highlands, assured me it is an old and oft repeated tale. She said it was passed along to her through her family, and that she liked to share it with as many people as possible every Christmas.

The story concerns the bells of a large church in another country, many years ago. These particular bells, hanging high in the church tower, were known for the rare beauty of their chimes. It was claimed they possessed the sweetest sound in all the world. Because the music was so beautiful, the bells never rang on ordinary days. Only on Christmas could they be heard.

It became a custom in that country for people to come from everywhere to the great church, with its wonderful bells. The people would bring generous offerings and lay them upon the altar. It was only at this moment of giving that the Christmas bells would begin to chime. Who rang them was unknown. It was said that mysterious, angelic hands pulled the bell rope, and the unique sound would float forth, filling the air with a lovely melody until the church was engulfed in an entrancing beauty.

Strangely enough, however, despite the great reputation of the bells, no living soul of the current generation had ever heard their music. Their lovely sound was known only by tradition, because for many years the bells had not rung. This was said to be due to the fact the people had become neglectful of the church and indifferent to God and seemed to care little for one another. The gift offerings had grown smaller each year, and nothing given in recent years had been enough to cause the bells to ring. Their beauty was remembered only in stories handed down from previous generations.

Eventually, the king of the land decided to do something about the bells' silence. He declared at the oncoming of the Christmas season that everyone should bring to the church the best and most generous gifts they could find. He said that he would personally bring his own gift to the church on Christmas Eve and await the bells to ring in Christmas day. Naturally, everyone planned to visit the city for this great event.

No one made plans more carefully than two little boys who lived a long distance from the city. Sons of a poor farm family, each somehow still managed to earn and save a small silver coin for an offering. Early on the afternoon of Christmas Eve, holding the coins tightly, they started their long walk to the city. It was bitterly cold, and they had not gone far before it started to snow heavily. Hand in hand, their shabby clothes wrapped tightly about them, they trudged on through the snow. The sun began to set quickly, and it was growing dark.

Suddenly, the older boy stumbled on an object huddled in the snow. Kneeling down to investigate, he was startled to find an old woman, nearly frozen but still alive. He lifted her and began to rub her wrists and temples. Her breathing grew more regular as the boy kept working with her, holding her close to his body and wrapping his arms around her. Meanwhile, the lights of the city shone in the distance, and large crowds could be seen converging toward the church.

The older boy, still holding the woman and rubbing her wrists and temples, looked up at his brother. "Go on to the church," he said, handing him his treasured bit of silver.

"Here's my offering. I must stay and do what I can to help this poor woman. When the church service is over, you can ask some people returning this way to help me with her."

The younger brother hesitated. "Go on," he was told. So the boy set off alone, clutching the two small pieces of silver in his hand. When he reached the church, it was very crowded and the ceremony had begun. Because he was small, the boy managed to squeeze his way through the crowd to find a place near the front where he could see the procession. People were already beginning to bring their gifts to the altar. The gifts grew richer and more impressive as time passed, but the bells remained silent.

Finally, the king himself stood at the altar, magnificent in his flowing robes and jewelry. With a dramatic gesture, he took his gold crown from his head and placed it on the altar. There was a hushed sigh from the congregation. Everyone waited expectantly. Surely the bells would ring for this gift. But the bells remained silent. Sadly, the king turned to walk down the aisle and leave the church. The people began to follow him.

Then, suddenly, from somewhere high in the tower, the most heavenly music began to ring out. The penetrating sound of the glorious Christmas bells filled the frosty air. The huge crowd stood like statues. Everyone looked back at the altar, but there was no one there. No one, that is, but a small boy, shyly placing two tiny silver coins on the altar, near the king's crown.

The Road We Traveled

Lena Penland Purkey was born in 1904 in Slabtown, a cove located in the Tennessee foothills of the Great Smoky Mountains. Lena vividly told me of her welcome to this world: "My reception was a cold one. It was bad enough to be born on a bleak, snowy day in January, the sixth child of an already overcrowded family; but to add insult to injury, my twelve-year-old half brother, Otto, took his foot in hand, as the old saying goes, and left home, loudly protesting, 'There are too many of us!'"

According to Lena, however, Otto's protest didn't bother the stork. It wasn't long before two more babies arrived. Otto never did come back. Lena's mother had first married a man from Finland who had come to America as a young man in search of adventure and a better way of life. Eventually, he migrated from New York down into the Southern Appalachians to work in the big timber of the Smokies. While working as a lumberjack, he met and married a seventeen-year-old girl, who one day would become Lena's mother.

"They were supremely happy," Lena said of the marriage. "But the warm, humid climate of the Southern Highlands proved too great a contrast to the ice and snow of his homeland. After a few years, he died of a fever, leaving my mother with four small children."

With a look of hurt in her eyes, as if she herself were experiencing the past agony, Lena related how her mother was compelled to sell the mountain farm left to her at her husband's death. Debts had piled up during the long illness. The widow made almost superhuman efforts to hold her family together, to keep food in their mouths, clothes on their backs, and a roof over their heads.

During this time Jim Penland came along. Known as a man of sterling character, he was a childless widower about fifty years old, and it was no secret that he was looking for a "good woman" to take as a wife. He owned a nice weatherboard house with acreage, so quite a number of women were interested in him. However, according to Lena, "Mama took the bull by the horns," and Mr. Penland gained a wife and four children. It was a good arrangement. However, Lena acknowledged that the generation gap was too wide, and that Mr. Penland remained almost a stranger in the household all his life.

Lena's mother was apparently a stranger to no one. She not only doctored and cared for her own brood, but was often called to tend to others who were suffering from some disease, experiencing pain from an accident, or laboring to give birth to a child. "The night was never too dark nor too late," Lena claimed. "Mama always went, taking simple dressings and supplies with her."

There was always a generous store of roots and herbs hanging from the porch rafters of the Penland house. "Mama was a strong believer in the use of home remedies," Lena explained. "She claimed there was nothing that could purify a body's blood like tea made from sassafras, yellow root, or wintergreen. And she always said that a brew made from blackberry roots was the best cure she ever knew of for 'summer complaint' (intestinal disturbance). And for a good night's sleep, a cup of hot tea made from the roots of wild lady's slippers would do the trick. Mama always told us that the good Lord put all these roots and herbs on earth to be used.

"In the spring, she would give every member of her family a big dose of sulfur and molasses. It was her 'sure cure' for spring fever. Of course, she always insisted that poke-sprout 'sallet' would serve the same purpose.

"If any of us got anything in our eyes, Mama put in a flax seed to chase it out. It worked, too. And she always insisted that earache could be relieved by blowing warm tobacco smoke into the ear. All minor cuts, bruises, and stubbed toes were doused with turpentine and then tied up with a clean white cloth.

"Mama thought pennyroyal tea was a cure for the hives, as well as for colic. She recommended 'teetering and tottering' to make a baby burp—and it works. Mama declared, 'It's good for babies to be juggled and bounced about. Keeps 'em from being liver bound.'"

Lena Penland Purkey liked to talk about her mother and the rest of her family, and of a time and way of life as it was once lived in the isolated coves of the Great Smoky Mountains. She enjoyed reflecting upon the past and sharing such reflections with others, because, in her words: "Unless we know where we came from, and something about the road we traveled as a people, how can we know who we are and where we're going?"

Thank you, Lena Penland Purkey.

Our Good
Will Find Us Out

This story I relate to you was told to me as the truth. I accept it as the truth because I have always heard that life is stranger than fiction. I have also been taught that our good will find us out. People have informed me that the story now has a life of its own and has been told as if the setting were places other than the Southern Highlands. However, I've had storytellers tell me that, without a doubt, it occurred right here.

The year was somewhere between 1903-1913. It was said to have been the coldest winter ever experienced in the mountains of East Tennessee. The temperature was near zero and falling as Tom Walker and Jack Colbert descended a peak in the Smokies one December afternoon. The two loggers, tired and weary, were on their way back to the Little River Lumber Company camp. Neither man was happy. They walked in silence. Someone had stolen their coats and gloves earlier that day, and they knew they must reach camp before dark to keep from literally freezing to death.

They had started the return trip later than planned. Already the sun was far to the west. The loggers' hands and feet were growing numb. Branches lashed against their faces as Walker and Colbert hurried through the trees and underbrush. Every now and then, the prolonged silence would be shattered by a loud swear as tree limbs cut the men's cheeks or gouged an eye and brought tears. The snow quieted their steps and clung to their boots and legs.

Colbert's mind reflected upon the past, scenes of the Great Lakes region he came from. He thought of the cold weather there and how he had always been prepared for it. He thought it was ironic that he would travel this far south to freeze to death. Walker was not a native of Tennessee either. He had grown up in the woods of Maine, moved to Pennsylvania, then followed the lumber company to these mountains to seek his fortune. Unexpectedly, he had fallen in love with a local girl, and they had already discussed marriage. He thought of her now, wondering if he would ever see her again.

It was then that they heard the groan and saw the man, a mound half-covered with snow. Badly hurt and semiconscious, he was barely able to move, unable to speak. Apparently, someone had also stolen his coat and gloves, as well as his boots.

Colbert and Walker brushed the snow from the man's body and examined him. It was evident he was near death. Colbert stood, looked down at the man, cupped his own freezing hands, and blew into them. He looked in the direction where camp should be. He then glanced back at Walker, who was still bending over the stranger.

"Ain't nothing we can do," Colbert said. "He's gonna die. That's for sure."

Walker looked up at Colbert. "We gotta do something," he replied. "We can't just leave him here."

The argument lasted for less than a minute. Colbert said it was senseless to waste valuable time. After telling Walker that he could do as he wished, Colbert turned from the pair. He pulled the collar of his wool shirt up against his neck and hastened away. Walker watched him disappear into the white trees and bushes. He then lifted the injured man and carefully placed him across his shoulders.

Walker's pace was now much slower. He struggled to catch up with Colbert, but Colbert was soon far out of sight. The sun set quickly, but the numbness which earlier had threatened to overtake Walker's body began to subside. Tiny beads of perspiration started to emerge above his top lip. Walker grew more tired, and the injured man seemed to become heavier. Walker had almost resigned to give way to complete exhaustion when he neared a clearing and saw the smoke rising from the lumber camp.

Walker's strength was renewed as he found within himself the power that accompanies the rebirth of hope. His pace quickened as he admired the beauty of the smoke pouring into the sky. In his excitement, however, he took his eyes off the path before him. He stumbled and fell, toppling from the weight on his shoulders. Lying in the snow, Walker became aware of the lifelessness of the man he had been carrying. He felt for the man's pulse, but there was none.

Walker slowly raised himself from the ground. For support, he placed his hand upon the snow-covered boulder that had caused him to trip. Surprisingly, it gave in to his weight. It was no boulder. It was Colbert, frozen to death. Walker suddenly realized that he had miraculously escaped the same fate. For the first time, he realized that the exertion from carrying the stranger had kept his own body warm and saved his life.

Female Ingenuity

The year was 1906. A group from Pennsylvania was planning to make a trip to settle near the sawmills just getting started in the mountains of East Tennessee. Ella and her husband had planned to be a part of the group, but Ella's husband died two weeks before the trip. Now the widow didn't know what to do. Most of the people in her area were making the journey, including all her friends, and Ella felt she would be all alone if she stayed in Pennsylvania. Finally, after much thought, she decided to cross the mountains.

Ella had a team of horses and a wagon, and she insisted that she would drive herself, because she was accustomed to the animals. By the time they neared the halfway point of the trek, however, a widower named Jacob had appointed himself as Ella's guardian, and he helped her with the driving along the way. Long before the trip ended in the Smokies, they had decided to marry.

When word got around about the upcoming marriage, all the members of the traveling group decided to give them a "commencement party," or wedding shower. So each family checked and rechecked possessions to see what they could find to present to the couple.

After the shower, some speculation arose as to whether or not there would be a minister to do the marrying when they arrived at the logging camp and sawmill. Some trappers passing on the trail stopped to visit and drink coffee, and they assured Ella and Jacob that the camp had a minister, one who had been quoted as saying, "There's enough sin in this camp to keep one preacher busy the rest of his life!"

Ella and Jacob were married the second day after their arrival in the Smokies, and work was begun on a log cabin that would become their home. However, the new life for Ella and Jacob, which seemed to start out so rosy, quickly took a turn for the worse as they began to experience their first winter in the mountains of East Tennessee.

Ella developed inflammatory rheumatism and was forced to take to her bed for many weeks. To make matters worse, Jacob found it necessary to leave her alone for most of the day as he journeyed to the mill and timber-cutting grounds where he worked from sunrise to sunset. Ella was unable to tend fires when her sickness was at its worst, but with plenty of bedding, she kept warm enough while Jacob was away.

Ella's confinement to bed, however, put some extra burdens upon Jacob. Among other things, day after day he attempted to make bread to go along with the little food they had to eat. Mixing it before he left for work, he would wrap it well, planning to bake it when he came home in the evening. It seldom worked, though. The fire usually went out in the small fireplace, and the cabin was simply too cold that winter for the dough to rise.

When both Ella and Jacob were about ready to give up having bread, Ella hit on the idea of having the bowl of bread dough tucked in beside her as she snuggled in bed to keep warm. The heat of her body kept the dough warm enough, and they began to have bread every evening.

After this success, Ella looked around for other ways of creatively utilizing her illness. In early spring, she asked Jacob to gather a few eggs from some of the neighbors who had chickens. He succeeded in getting two dozen, and Ella put them in the bed with her. Keeping the eggs close to her body, turning and shifting them as carefully as ever a mother hen could do, twenty-three fluffy yellow chicks were hatched. By that time, Ella was improved enough to get up and care for her brood.

That first winter became the foundation of the long-lasting relationship between Ella and Jacob. As the years passed, Ella continued to meet problem situations head-on, usually creatively turning such situations into positive results.

Flowers Spring From Strange Places

Elias Covington had been a preacher at one time, but now, in the early 1900s, he had settled down on the eastern fringe of the Smoky Mountains to work as a blacksmith, and he was doing quite well. One spring evening, however, three mountaineer farmers and their wives brought a challenge to his house.

"We've got us a church building, and we've got us a congregation," the leader of the group told Elias, "but we don't have no preacher." Looking at Elias steadily, the man asked, "Will you be our pastor?"

Elias just stared at him, looked at the others, and then asked the leader, "How many members do you have?"

"Six," the man replied. "You're a-lookin' at the whole congregation right now." Elias studied his potential church members, taking special notice of the determined and hopeful look in their eyes.

The leader of the group spoke again. "We've each pledged a dollar a week fer yore salary. That's six dollars a week." He paused, glanced at the others, then asked, "When do you want to start?"

Elias took the chance. He loved to preach and missed it dearly; the last church he served had closed when all the members either died or moved away. He decided that this time, through the leadership of God, his own determination, and the support of these six members, this church would grow and prosper rather than die.

Elias's task wasn't easy. Newcomers were moving into the area as many of the old residents moved west or passed away. Many of the new inhabitants were emigrants who distrusted people they didn't know and were wary of people who tried to Americanize them. Some didn't like the church because they thought the church didn't like them. Elias began to hunt for new members so his church might grow. Upon his first visit to a prospective family, he ran into trouble.

Seeing the minister's old black hat, rusty coat, and Bible tucked under his arm as he approached, a farmer yelled for his dogs. As Elias marched implacably toward him, the farmer screamed, "Religion! Bad stuff! Bad stuff! Get out of here!" With a pitchfork in hand, the farmer advanced toward Elias.

Elias pivoted on his heels and started back in the direction he had come from, but he took a wrong turn and pulled up short on the brink of a manure pit. Cornered there, he turned to face the farmer and held up his hands, tightly clutching the old, worn Bible high above his head. The farmer kept coming with his pitchfork. He was a man of immense bulk, weighing about 300 pounds, but Elias didn't have any notion of trying to run past him.

The farmer had addressed Elias with a pronounced German brogue, so the minister, on the brink of the manure pit and hemmed in by a charging pitchfork propelled by a 300-pound man, called upon God and upon his wits. "Praise be to Martin Luther!" Elias shouted. "And thank heaven for German sugar beets!" he continued. "And long live King William!"

The farmer skidded to a halt and lowered his pitchfork. "Bernice," the farmer said, turning to face his wife, who had been following the chase, "he is a friend. Get him some cold milk."

Elias lowered his arms and wiped the sweat from his brow. He kissed the Bible still tightly clutched in his other hand.

Elias enjoyed his milk in the German farmhouse, and he asked about the couple's young daughter, who hummed softly as she packed some eggs in a basket for Elias.

"Liska does have a musical voice," the farmer responded.

"Does she sing?" Elias asked. "The people at our church would love to hear her."

"She should never believe in the religious stuff you say in America," the farmer replied. "But to show she can sing, why not? Yes, she can sing to your people."

Elias also found a German violinist. A woman from Scotland was discovered to have a beautiful alto voice. A Dutch emigrant, recently down from Pennsylvania, was proud of his woodworking talent and shared it with the church, remodeling the old building inside and out as he recruited others to help.

The church grew and prospered, getting its start that day when Elias tenaciously balanced himself on the edge of the manure pit while facing an oncoming pitchfork. Flowers spring from strange places.

A Little Help From My "Friends"

I began collecting stories from native old-timers in the mid-1970s, a few years after I moved to Gatlinburg. Some of my so-called "friends" heard of my endeavors. They told me of an elderly man who lived way back up in the mountains and would be a perfect resource for me. I thanked them, got directions on how to get to the cabin, and then set aside a day for the trip.

On the chosen day, I drove as far as I could following the given directions, then walked about a mile, finally reaching my destination and the elderly man. He was sitting in a rocking chair on his front porch, reading the local weekly newspaper through his bifocals. This surprised me, because I just didn't think about someone that far up in the mountains reading a newspaper.

I introduced myself and told him I was collecting stories. He responded by saying, "Oh, yeah, you that young feller that talks a lot, ain'tcha?"

"Yes sir," I responded, surprised again, this time at his knowledge of me. "I do speak to some groups."

He looked me over. "You talk a whole lot, don'tcha? And you write stuff?"

Well, apparently he had read in the paper about some of the

conferences at which I had spoken and had read some of the columns I had written for the paper.

"Yes sir," I confessed. "I guess I do talk a whole lot. And I do write some."

"Well, young feller," he said, "I've got a story with a moral that will fit you just right."

"That's great," I told him as I got out my pencil and paper. "Let's hear it."

He proceeded to relate this story:

"One day, a wild bull stepped out of the woods and into a clearing. At about that same time, a mountain lion stepped out of the woods on the other side of the clearing. They stared at each other and started circling around the clearing, keeping their eyes steadily fixed on one another.

"Suddenly, they charged. For a while, it looked like the mountain lion would get the best of the bull. Then it looked like the bull would get the best of the mountain lion.

"For hours on end, they fought. Finally, the mountain lion saw an opening, leapt up, grabbed the bull by the throat, sank his fangs into the bull, and killed him. The mountain lion was filled with pride, but he was also hungry, since they had been struggling all day. The mountain lion thought to himself, *I have defeated this bull, and now I will devour him.* He proceeded to do just that, leaving nothing but the horns and the hooves.

"Exceptionally proud of himself, the mountain lion pranced up to the top of the highest peak in the area, surveyed his vast domain, threw back his head, and roared.

"About that time, a hunter, who had been hunting all day and had not shot a thing, heard the mountain lion. He looked up and saw the lion perched on the mountain peak, framed by the sunset. The hunter carefully put his rifle to his shoulder, took solid aim, squeezed the trigger, hit the lion in the head, and killed him."

"That's it?" I asked.

"Yep, young feller, that's it."

I was puzzled. "Well, where's the moral?" I asked. "Where's the moral that you said would fit me just right?"

With a twinkle in his eye, the old mountaineer said, "Young feller, the moral of that story is, When you are full of bull, keep your mouth shut."

A Different Type of Help

Several different people have told me versions of this story, which supposedly occurred in the late 1800s in the Smokies. Maybe something similar happened on numerous occasions. Whatever the case, it is good example of another way in which the mountaineers helped one another.

Little Jimmy Suttles and his father, Oren Suttles, were sitting in front of the fireplace in their cabin. Jimmy's mother, his little brother, and his three sisters had already gone to bed in the loft. Jimmy and his father watched the pork meat, packed just the right way, roasting in the back of the fire.

The night was bitter. They could hear rain pelting on the wooden roof and feel the wind as it howled across the front porch of the cabin. Nights such as this gave eight-year-old Jimmy the creeps and caused him to conjure up all types of evils lurking out in the woods.

Suddenly, Jimmy and his father heard hooves splash in the puddles formed in front of the porch. Wide-eyed, Jimmy turned to look at his father. It was later than he usually stayed up, and Jimmy knew that people would never call this time of night unless it was a dire emergency. He wasn't surprised when his father reached for his loaded shotgun. Jimmy stood by his father and listened as someone dismounted, tied up his mount, and stepped up on the porch.

There was a tap on the door, followed by a rather soft,

"Oren? Oren? You up?" Jimmy and his father exchanged glances. They recognized the voice.

"Buford?" Oren Suttles responded. "That you, Buford?"

"Yeah," the man outside answered. "It's me all right." Buford's voice was pitched higher than usual. Oren put down his shotgun, stepped toward the entrance, lifted the latch, and opened the door.

Buford Gibson, a neighbor from down the creek, stood on the porch, soaking wet, with a wild look in his big eyes. Rain ran off the brim of his felt hat and dropped off the end of his long nose. His drenched coat, filled with goose down, was probably doing more to keep him cold than to keep him warm.

"Put your mule in the barn, Buford, and come on in," Oren said.

Buford shook his head. "I can't stay long, Oren. I just need to talk to you a minute." His eyes remained wild.

"Sure," Oren responded. "Come on in." Oren looked at Jimmy, knowing that the frightful look on Buford's face was probably scaring the boy. "Come set a spell."

Buford walked into the room, nodded a slight acknowledgment at little Jimmy, and then looked back at Oren. He walked over to the fireplace and stretched his bony fingers toward the fire for warmth. He stared into the flickering light, then turned to face Oren.

"Oren," Buford said shakily. "Oren, I'm a-gonna die."

Oren looked at Buford, glanced toward Jimmy and then back at Buford, and said, "We all gonna die, Buford. The Bible says we all gonna die someday."

"I mean now," Buford said, more loudly than before. Oren looked toward the loft. Buford glanced up as well and, realizing the family was in bed, spoke more softly, but with urgency. "I just came up on that big oak where I turn to go to my place. My mule stopped in his tracks, laid his ears back against his head, and then the whole area lit up with lightning."

Buford paused. Oren didn't say anything, waiting for the frightened man to continue his story.

Buford took a deep breath, looked at Jimmy, and then at Oren. "I seen my coffin, Oren. I seen my coffin sure as shootin'—and I was a-layin' in it!"

Oren still didn't speak. Of course, little Jimmy was all ears and eyes.

"You know what that means, don't you, Oren? It means I'm gonna die. It means I'm gonna die afore morning!"

All the ghost stories little Jimmy had ever heard couldn't top this! He was afraid of ghosts, but he knew they were only stories. But now he thought, *This is really happening!*

Oren walked over, picked up the poker from the hearth, and stirred the fire. Then he turned toward Buford and calmly said, "I've heard the same thing, Buford, but I don't set much store in such matters." He placed the poker back on the hearth.

"You don't?" Buford responded to Oren's calm statement. His eyes seemed to lose some of their wildness.

"Heavens, no," Oren continued. "Why, if I've seen my coffin one time, I've seen it a dozen."

"Yeah?" Buford said hopefully. "You really seen yore coffin afore?"

"Through the years," Oren assured him, "at least a dozen times."

Buford's big eyes brightened, and he broke out in a grin. "Well, don't that beat all," he declared. "Don't that beat all!" Oren nodded his head and returned the smile.

Buford looked toward Jimmy, then up toward the loft, saying, "Well, I best be a-goin'. It's late and I got a piece ta ride."

Oren walked Buford to the door and lifted the latch. On the way out, Buford paused in the entranceway, looked back at Oren, and said, "You know, there in my coffin I had on a brand-new blue suit, and I really looked good. 'Bout the best I ever looked, I guess!"

Oren and Buford exchanged good-byes, then Buford untied his mule, mounted it, and rode away a happy man. Oren shut the door and lowered the latch. He turned toward Jimmy.

Jimmy's eyes were as wide as Buford's had been earlier. "Pa?" he asked. "Have you really seen your coffin?"

"No, son," Oren responded as he rubbed Jimmy's hair. "And Buford didn't see one tonight, neither. But don't ever tell Buford—or anyone else."

Jimmy looked up at his father. "But. . . ."

Oren interrupted. "Buford's a good man, son. But sometimes he gets strange ideas. Sort of gets funny in the head. If what I told him made him feel better, so be it." The father and son exchanged knowing glances, then got ready to go up to bed.

Kate's Miracle

It was my good fortune to speak with a lady nearing 100 years of age who was born and reared near Townsend, Tennessee. She was the one who told me about Kate.

Kate's husband had been killed in 1904 in a sawmill accident, and she was left with four small children, very little money, and rather poor health. She supported herself and the children by taking in washing for the unmarried loggers and cooking for the lumber company when she was able. When she was too sick to work, no money would come in for food and other family needs. Through it all, however, Kate was known as the most devout Christian in the area. It seemed that the harder things became for Kate, the more her faith grew.

Most people admired such faith, but Horace Davis ridiculed it. Davis was the meanest man in the mountains. He was known for his vile language, his excessive drinking, and for his knack of getting into fights over the least little thing. It was also commonly agreed upon that Davis was the most powerful lumberjack who had ever swung an ax in the Southern Appalachians.

If there was one thing Davis detested the most, it was religion. He didn't like to talk about religion, and he didn't like to hear anyone else talk about it. That's why he started harassing Kate one night when she was serving supper at the lumber company.

"How you doin', Kate?" one of the other loggers had inquired as the frail woman placed some mashed potatoes on the table.

"The Lord's been good to me," Kate answered with a glowing smile.

Davis winced at her words. "Good to ya, huh?" he taunted. "And has your Lord performed any miracles for you today?"

"Miracles are happening all the time, Horace," Kate replied calmly. Davis threw back his head and roared with laughter at Kate's straightforward answer. He punched a couple of cohorts in their ribs to encourage them to join in. "Then how 'bout askin' your Lord to send me one, Kate—if He's got any extra!" Davis shouted through his laughter. Most of the other men were rather quiet, impressed by Kate's composure.

Three weeks later, a tree fell on Davis. It broke his back and tore up some of his internal organs. At first, the company doctor didn't think Davis would live. Later, when the rough lumberjack did actually make it through, the doctor said he would never walk again, but he did. When he was able to be up and around, some of the men told him about Kate's praying.

"The doc said you was gonna' die for sure," one man told Davis. "But Kate, she said no. She said she done prayed 'bout it, and the Lord done tole her that this was gonna be yore miracle."

The people in the logging camp and surrounding area talked about Davis's miracle—how he was almost killed, how he lived when the doctor said he would die, and how he walked again when the doctor said it would be impossible. But the big topic centered around Kate's miracle. People discussed how Davis discarded his old vocabulary and acquired a new one, how he changed his drinking habits, how his fights became few and far between—and how he cared for his new wife, Kate, and their children.

The Roamin' Man of the Mountains

When I moved to Gatlinburg in the early 1970s, I often talked with Casey Oakley and listened to his stories. Casey is a rare character. His father, Wiley, was even rarer. Wiley Oakley was born in the mountains of East Tennessee, near Gatlinburg, on September 12, 1885, and was later known as "The Roamin' Man of the Mountains." People came from all over the nation to hear his tales and to hire him to be their guide in the Great Smoky Mountains.

Always a dreamer and idealist, Wiley was the youngest of eleven or twelve children born to Henry and Elmina Oakley. The exact number of children is unknown, because Wiley always said, "Thar was eight boys an' three girls that I knowed of—but thar may a-been 'nother boy."

As the youngest child, Wiley was extremely close to his mother, and when she died while he was still just a small boy, Wiley refused to be comforted. Seeking to assure him that his mother was in good hands, some relatives told Wiley that his mother was not really dead. They explained that she had become an angel, with a white robe and a starry crown, living in heaven with God. They told Wiley that if he were a good boy, he could join his mother again some day.

Little Wiley, however, did not want to wait that long to see his mother again. He began to wander away from the family's cabin, looking up toward heaven, searching for his mother. Eventually, he imagined certain cloud formations to be his mother's robe. Lying on his back one evening, gazing up at the stars, he saw a bright constellation, which he felt must be his mother's crown. He spoke to the stars, and he later told how the stars twinkled back at him at that very moment.

The day after seeing his mother's "crown," little Wiley left the cabin early, without telling anyone, and set off for the tallest peak in the mountains. He was sure if he climbed high enough, he would be able to touch his mother's robe, to get one of the stars from her crown, and maybe even get a chance to talk with her face-to-face.

Late that evening, his worried family finally located the runaway boy, who was tired, hungry, and ragged with briar scratches. Wiley was scolded and soundly spanked. He was also admonished to never pull such a trick again. However, as Wiley revealed years later, he continued to make secret visits to the mountain peaks to seek his mother.

The searches for his mother eventually made him a daily companion of the mountains. As he grew older, the searches became expeditions through the woods and by the streams, through the valleys and atop the peaks. Later, Wiley said the only two possessions he had during his "growin'-up" years were a dog and a rifle. With these by his side, he spent his days roaming, fishing, and hunting.

By the time Wiley was a teenager, he had roamed just about every inch of the Smokies, every place any human had been before as well as places no one had ever seen. It is no wonder that Wiley became the person to guide people on hikes and take them hunting and fishing in the Great Smoky Mountains.

As Wiley grew into young manhood, his brothers and sisters were all getting married and leaving home, so Wiley decided it might be time to find a bride. There were areas where the mountain people would make sorghum molasses in autumn. In the evenings at such locations, the boys and girls would "pull candy" and make wishes.

According to Wiley, this was a good place for a boy to find girls and to "cast sheep eyes" at the girl he liked best. When a boy cast sheep eyes, the girl would cast them back with a nice smile if she was interested in him. However, if the girl returned a "sour look" instead, Wiley said, "You best call yore dogs an' go home, fer the fox race was over with." You would just have to try again with someone else later on.

"One night I found a girl," Wiley declared. She gave him a smile, "casting the sheep eye" back to him. He walked Dorothy home that night and several times after that.

"Finally," Wiley said, "Dorothy askt me ter come visit her on a Saturday evenin'." A Saturday-evening visit was a very important event. Wiley cleaned up and dressed early that Saturday, getting over to the girl's house by 4:00 P.M.

As Wiley explained it, "A little boy met me near her cabin door an' tole me ter go 'way 'cause Dorothy had 'nother beau a-callin' on her that evenin'."

Wiley was heartbroken, but he was also afraid that Dorothy would tell all the other girls how she had "broken his leg." This phrase was used when a girl turned a boy down, meaning she had rejected him by kicking him in the shin. Wiley went home that Saturday evening and decided he would be better off if he just forgot about courting and marrying and such. He determined he would be better off with just his dog and rifle.

Later, however, Wiley decided that Dorothy's action had not ruined him for life. He came to the conclusion that he would try again. His thinking was, "Iffen I git kicked again, hit ain't no big thing, since I already been kicked afore."

Wiley discovered that Dorothy had been nice enough not to tell any of the other girls she had "kicked" him. As a matter of fact, on the way home from hunting one day, he ran into Dorothy. She apologized to him, and said she would like to make up with him. She invited Wiley to come visit her again.

Wiley said, "I tole her I would haf ter think hit over 'cause I had 'nother girl at the time who lived 'bout ten miles on t'other side of the mountain." Wiley, indeed, was seeing a girl who lived about ten miles away. He thought Dorothy had told all the local girls about kicking him, so he wanted to go far enough to find someone who would not laugh at him.

After discovering Dorothy had not spread the word about him, Wiley decided to find a local girl so he wouldn't have to go so far to "do some courtin'." However, as Wiley described it, "At a little log cabin church house one Sunday, I went up ter a girl an' askt her iffen I could walk her home. She didn't say nary word, jist up an' kicked me on my leg, then turned round an' left. An' I jist stood thar a-thinkin', 'Now I done been kicked twice!'"

Wiley felt he was getting immune to being kicked, so he just went up to another girl and asked her if he could walk her home. "She said yes," Wiley explained. "So right then an' thar I found out thar was plenty of girls ter go round."

Later, however, Wiley decided he could live without the girls. In his words, "I became as independent as a hog on ice. I 'cided to give up on all the girls, a-thinkin' I was too young ter git married an' also 'cidin' thar was more fun in huntin' an' ramblin' the woods, an', also, that I should know more 'bout the outer world since I had been out of the mountains very little." Wiley got out of the mountains some, but not very far and not for very long.

Back in the mountains, at the age of nineteen, Wiley "got the hankerin'" to see girls again. He fell for fifteen-year-old Rebecca Ann Ogle, his "beautiful, golden-haired, brown-eyed sweetheart." They decided to get married, so Wiley obtained a license, expecting to have the wedding in a few days. Wiley was proud of this "official paper" he held in his hand, so he decided to visit Rebecca Ann that evening and show it to her.

The couple went for a stroll in the moonlight. On their way

back to Rebecca Ann's home, Wiley looked up at the sky and said, "See that moon? See those stars? Why wait ter git hitched? Why not tonight?"

Rebecca Ann was surprised, to say the least. Wiley said, "I know a preacher man acrost the mountain. Let's go git the knot tied now!"

The pair trekked across the mountain, hand in hand. Within an hour, Wiley knocked on the door at the mountain minister's cabin.

"Who's thar?" came the voice from inside.

"The Roamin' Man of the Mountains," Wiley replied, "An' I'm a-wantin' to git married."

"When?" the voice from within responded.

"Now!" Wiley shouted.

There was a pause, then the minister yelled out, "I'm in bed!"

"Well," Wiley reasoned, "can't you git up?"

There was another pause. "Yes," the minister answered. "But hit's late—and we'uns is all in bed—and the fire is kivered. Ye can't come in."

Wiley looked at Rebecca Ann. There was silence. Then the minister spoke again.

"Ye got the gal with ye?" he asked.

"Yep," Wiley called back.

"Ye got the paper?"

"Yep," Wiley said again.

"Ye got a dollar cash money?"

"Yep," Wiley answered for the third time.

The minister then instructed Wiley to "slide the paper and the dollar under the door, and you'uns stand up out thar and join hands." Standing in the moonlight outside the cabin door, with the minister conducting the ceremony from within, Wiley and Rebecca Ann were united in holy matrimony.

Wiley always claimed that they "got hitched by an invisible preacher man." Later, Wiley's fame spread, and he was offered a national network radio show originating from New York, a show on which he could spin his yarns and tell his tales. Some local people warned him that if he accepted the offer and went to New York, his wife would divorce him.

To this, Wiley always replied, "Divorce! Why, she can't even prove she's married ter me. She never saw the preacher!" Wiley never accepted the radio-show offer; even though he came close to doing so, he just couldn't imagine leaving the Great Smoky Mountains. Tapes of his stories, however, were played over the airwaves.

The couple had a good life together. In Wiley's words, there were a few "squawls" in the course of their marriage, but never a "tempest" that couldn't be handled. They also brought twelve children into this world. An event with some of the children is the focus of one of Wiley's famous stories:

"We'uns had been a-livin' on Scratch Britches Mountain fer 'bout four years," Wiley explained. "One summer day, Mrs. Wiley had gone ter Gatlinburg ter do some tradin' while I kept house an' looked after the boys. I 'cided ter work a little round the house, an' I put the boys on a quilt out in the yard, whar I could keep an eye on 'em while I was a-cleanin' out some weeds.

"All at once, I heerd a rattlesnake a-singin'. I looked ter see whar hit was, an' saw hit near one o' the boys. He was a-crawlin' toward the snake, an' hit was a-coiled ter strike 'im.

"I rushed ter the boy, caught 'im, an' jerked 'im away. I then got the hoe an' chopped off the snake's head.

"When Mrs. Wiley came home, I told her 'bout what had happened an' how close the boy came ter gettin' bit. Hit scared her, but, of course, we both jist figgered the snake had crawled in from the nearby woods.

"That very night, though, Mrs. Wiley was a-washin' some things in the kitchen, when she called out ter me ter come into the kitchen at once. When I ran ter see what she wanted, she jist looked at me an' said, 'Listen.' We both heerd a rattlesnake a-singin'. I thought at first hit was in the house, but soon 'cided hit was under the floor.

"Well, hit was dark outside, too dark ter crawl up under the house ter kill a snake. So I figgered out whar hit was under the kitchen floor an' poured some boilin' water down a crack. But the more we'uns poured, the more snakes we heerd a-singin'.

"Finally, we 'cided the best thing ter do was ter plug up any holes or cracks the snakes might could crawl through ter get into the house. Then we 'cided ter go ter bed an' wait till daylight. Hit certainly wouldn't be safe ter go out into the dark after pouring water on 'em an' a-gettin' 'em mad. We left candles burnin' all night, so we'uns could see the snakes, just in case some of 'em got into the house.

"The next mornin', we'uns got up a-lookin' all round the house. We'uns didn't spot no snakes. Then, I went ter the door an' looked very carefully into the yard afore I went outside. I walked around ter the back of the house an' looked ter see iffen I could locate any dead snakes, but didn't find nary a one.

"Then I saw a big holler log rolled up under the kitchen where we'uns had poured the water. So I got a stick an' poked in the log. Hit sounded like a hundred snakes started a-singin'.

"We 'cided ter move away an' turn the cabin over ter the snakes, an' so we did."

Wiley's greatest talent lay in his storytelling, but he also wrote poetry, painted, and was extremely fond of music. He always carried a "mouth organ," or harmonica, with him, but, according to Wiley, "The thing I like best is ter jist set an' listen ter brook music. Brook music beats book music."

Wiley never "took ter book learnin'," but he guided scholars in unforgettable mountain excursions. They would always return from the trips talking more about the man who led them than the sights they had experienced. A wealthy businessman once said of Wiley, "He's the richest man I know, because of his rare philosophy of life and his ability to enjoy everything that surrounds him every day!"

Some of Wiley's philosophies this wealthy businessman referred to include:

- The world is already made. We'uns can't make hit over. When hit gits too much fer you, try a-goin' off ter some quiet mountain peak an' a-lookin' down on the world with all hits troubles an' cares, an' then see iffen hit matters. That's the way I do. I jist wander off by myself, way up high in the hills, an' look down on the ole Earth and say, "Let 'er spin."
- Don't complain. People ain't a-gonna like you iffen yore always a-grouchin'. They like ter do the grouchin' theirselves.
- Faultin' others don't git you nowheres—exceptin' in trouble.
- There ain't no such thing as being perfect, but you can be very good in one thing iffen you make hit a study.
- Be as honest as you can, even though you may make many mistakes in life.
- When you find yoreself off the trail that leads ter God and ter that happy place He has built fer his people, stop, look, and listen. Try ter git back on the trail again.
- Use plain ole common sense in all things. Common sense is hard ter beat.
- If you will do the best you can whilst traveling through this life, hit will go well in the future.
- Today is a day. Tonight is a night. An' tomorrow is just another day. So why should people worry 'bout a few minutes, like so many people do?
- Money don't mean much ter me. Iffen you have money, somebody is always after you, tryin' ter git it away from you. Quite a few people askt me why I don't take that radio offer and make me a lot o' money. I'm afraid they don't understand the trouble in the ideer of agreein' to talk when

other people want me ter talk and agreein' fer sich a long period of time. Hits a mighty long time ter make a little money an' haf ter be on the dot ter a minute when I do hit. This jist don't appeal ter me, not in the slightest degree. I say, do what you like ter do in order ter be happy, rather than doing what somebody else wants you ter do and thinks you should do ter be happy.

• Faith is what's left in you after yore plumb broke down and give out. But the Book says, "Faith will move a mountain."

Wiley Oakley left this world on November 18, 1954. His legacy still lives in the Great Smoky Mountains, and his philosophy is still appreciated by scholars and non-scholars alike.

Gumption, Guts, and Grit!

In the autumn of 1907, when Lena Penland Purkey was three years old and living in Slabtown, Tennessee, her parents faced a momentous decision. They had the opportunity to swap farms with a man living in Lost Creek, North Carolina. Although the farm lay only about twenty miles across the mountains, it seemed like the other side of the world.

When Lena's mother was first approached with the subject of moving, she replied, "Law, yes, I'm willin' to pull stakes and go over the mountain to Carolina. It can't be any rougher over there than 'tis here. Besides, I've heard a lot o' talk 'bout that good school the Presbyterians opened up at Hot Springs. And there's one thing for certain, I aim for my children to have a better chance for schoolin' than I ever had."

Lena said her mother had never had more than a year's schooling, "all told." Yet Lena claimed that her mother was familiar with the *McGuffey Readers,* often quoting passages from them and from the Bible. Her mother had spelled through the *Blue Back Speller* and wrote in a "neat, spidery hand." She constantly urged Lena and the other children "to get an education and be somebody." Lena's mother insisted, "Nothin's impossible for a body that's got gumption, guts, and grit!"

Lena and her family left Tennessee for North Carolina on a bright October morning. No one in the family had ever seen Lost Creek. They had simply swapped farms, sight unseen. The only description they had of their new home was "one hundred acres of fairly rolling land." Lena's father guided their two strapping oxen, Mike and Baldy, across the log-and-plank bridge that spanned Big Creek, which ran in front of their Slabtown home, and headed them down the stream.

The oxen's wooden yoke creaked and groaned, as did the wagon under its heavy load. Lena said she was later told how her mother took a last long look at the little white weatherboard house that she had been so proud of, for it was one of the few painted houses in Slabtown. Then firmly setting her face forward, she said "Pshaw. No use lookin' back. Let's look ahead."

Lena rode in a featherbed nestled among the household goods. The rest of the family walked, even pushed when necessary. William and Hubert, the two oldest boys, led the procession, driving the two milk cows, Spot and Daisy. Papa followed, prodding the oxen, while Mama, along with Flora, Willie, and Jimmie, brought up the rear.

Lena's mother told her later that the whole family was in high spirits on that moving day. She explained to her that it was a good feeling to be moving, even if none of them was quite sure just what they were moving to. When she was about seventy, in the mid to late 1970s, Lena was assisted in polishing the visual description her mother had given her many years earlier.

She shared that description with me in this manner: "It was a blue gold Indian Summer day. The air was like wine; wild aster were blooming in profusion along the road banks. The hills were aglow with the red and yellow leaves of autumn trees, fodder shocks stood like small wigwams on the little hillside farms, and yellow pumpkins and squash sprawled in naked abandon among the corn stubble. The river babbled a merry tune as it swirled and flowed over and around the big boulders lying in its pathway."

The procession followed Big Creek down to the little station of Del Rio. There, they turned eastward along the narrow dirt road that followed close beside the rocky French Broad River and the railroad that had come to the area in 1869. At Wolf Creek, near the Tennessee/North Carolina line, the family turned away from the railroad and the narrow river valley. They drove past the old Allen Inn, which for so long had been a haven for the early stock drovers. From there, they followed the old stagecoach road that led them to their new Carolina home. Lena claimed that even though she was only three at the time, she would carry forever a hazy recollection of the oxen straining and stalling as they climbed "rock-cliff hill," in sight of the new home.

The house on Lost Creek, according to Lena, was a typical mountain home. It consisted of scalped logs and a mud-daubed "chimley," and was covered with hand-split shingles. The doors were made of wide hand-planed planks, and they were opened and closed with wooden latches. Lena said the house was not as good nor half as comfortable as the one the family had in Tennessee, but the location was better. It stood on a little knoll in the center of the farm, circled by a rim of blue mountains.

"It was a beautiful, wide-open place to live," Lena said as she closed her eyes and reflected upon childhood. There was silence before she spoke again, her eyes now open, sparkling, like those of a child on Christmas morning. She handed me a paper on which she, with assistance, had labored, hoping one day to include it in her memoirs.

She told me that she had sought help in getting the words just right: "In the brooding quiet of early evening, we could hear the distant pounding of the driver of the steam locomotive and listen to the lonesome wail of its whistle ricocheting against the hills. That moaning, wailing whistle, which filled us with such longing, was engineer Mike O'Conner's signal to the hill folk, as he opened the throttle and let Old Number 'Leven roll down the narrow gorge of the French Broad River. For the moment, we were lost in awe and wonder, gripped with a nameless longing for faraway places. We had a wild desire to go and see for ourselves what lay out there beyond the rim of the mountains."

Lena's mother and her experience at Lost Creek inspired her to become a teacher. With her mother's words often echoing in her ears, Lena got an education and "became somebody." She often recalled her mother's words: "Nothin's impossible for a body that's got gumption, guts, and grit!"

Jessie Hargrove

When Jessie Hargrove was born in the early 1900s, his mother didn't like him. She never wanted him in the first place. Jessie's father had run off with another woman, leaving his wife to have the baby on her own. When Jessie grew from babyhood to childhood and began to look more and more like his father, his mother liked him even less. "Look at him!" his mother would exclaim, embarrassing him in front of neighbors and friends. "Why in the world would God make two of 'em?"

The rest of the community treated Jessie much like his mother did. He seemed never to smile, and he couldn't talk without stuttering. When he finally started school, approaching his teenage years, no one expected him to last very long with his books. He lived up to their expectations. At age fourteen, Jessie dropped out of school and began picking up odd jobs in the Smoky Mountain community he called home.

Jessie had always worked, but now he was excited about the fact that he was going to get paid for it. He had grown up chopping wood, drawing water for his mother's washings, plowing their small, mountaintop farm, and running all the errands his mother could find to keep him out of her sight.

Jessie was soon much in demand as hired help throughout the community. His great strength, his dependability, and the fact that he was never "distracted by girls" made him a

104

sought-after commodity. His mother was overjoyed at the wages he started bringing in. The extra work, along with his usual duties around his own home and farm, kept him out of his mother's sight more than ever. Jessie's absence was almost as pleasing to her as the money.

Shortly after Jessie's sixteenth birthday, his mother caught pneumonia. Jessie took care of her, nursing her faithfully, but she didn't respond to his careful treatment. Two months after her sickness began, she died, leaving Jessie alone. Jessie was sixteen, but he looked thirty-five. The dawn-to-sunset work, his obligations around the house, and, finally, the last two months of taking care of his mother had aged him.

He did a good job taking over the farm. He had done most of the work for years, but now he made some changes and initiated some things he had learned while working on other farms in the area.

Around this time, a recession hit the Smoky Mountains area. Money had never been abundant in Jessie's community, but now it was far less available than ever before. It appeared that Jessie couldn't hire himself out anymore, since the farmers didn't have the money to pay him.

Jessie came up with an idea, suggesting to the farmers they could pay him in other ways. Jessie's pay came in the form of some cows from a couple of farmers and some feed from another. One farmer sliced off a piece of his land that adjoined Jessie's small farm and gave him the land in return for his help. In time, Jessie's farm grew, and so did his belongings.

Before long, a young lady entered Jessie's life. She was the daughter of the minister who had just moved to town. The minister, not knowing that Jessie had never attended church because his mother was against it, came to visit Jessie and invited him to attend a Sunday meeting. Unaware of Jessie's background, the minister did not look upon Jessie as the rest of the community had always done. Rather, he saw him as an industrious young farmer who seemed to have good ideas.

At first, Jessie was afraid of the minister's invitation. No one had ever asked him to come to church before. After the initial shock wore off, however, Jessie became excited, and he accepted the invitation.

That first Sunday at church, Jessie met Dawn, the minister's daughter. Several weeks later, they actually talked with each other. In a little over a month, Jessie ate Sunday dinner with Dawn and her family. Shortly thereafter, another dinner engagement was followed by a ride in Jessie's horse-drawn wagon. Jessie and Dawn began to see one another more often. Having been schooled, Dawn frequently would accompany Jessie and read to him as he plowed or worked with the livestock or attended to numerous other chores around his farm and the farms of others.

Shortly after his twentieth birthday, Jessie married Dawn. The once-bland house that had always been Jessie's home took on a new look as Dawn dressed it up. Jessie began to smile a lot, and everyone seemed to forget how Jessie used to stutter. His farm had now grown so much and his livestock had multiplied so greatly that he had to quit working for other farmers. He hired someone to help him.

By the time Jessie was twenty-five, farmers were flocking to him, respecting the answers he gave to their questions. They asked about ways to plant crops, how to care for livestock, and how to make the most out of financial resources. A few years later, it came as no surprise to anyone when Jessie was chosen as the first president of the first bank in this Smoky Mountain community.

Ernie's Story

Ernie often told of how he had a dreadful horror of snakes when he was a boy—a horror that followed him into adulthood. It wasn't that he was afraid of being killed by a snake. He just had an unusually strong desire to get away from the reptiles, whether it might be a six-inch garden snake or a six-foot rattler.

When Ernie was just a little fellow, maybe four or five, his father was plowing at the far end of their farm, and Ernie was walking along behind the plow, barefooted in the fresh soft furrow. His father had just started the field and was plowing near a weedy fencerow where wild roses were growing.

Ernie asked his father for his pocketknife so the young boy could cut some of the roses to take back to his mother. His father gave him the knife and went on plowing. Ernie sat down in the grass and started cutting off the roses.

Suddenly, a blue racer came looping through the grass at Ernie. He screamed, dropped the knife, and ran from the scene as fast as he could. Ernie then remembered that the knife was his father's. He crept back over the plowed ground and searched the area until he found it. Ernie's father had heard the wild, animallike scream and had stopped his plowing. Ernie returned the knife to his father, assured him everything was all right, and started back to the house.

Ernie approached the house from the west side, where

there was an old garden grown up in high weeds. He stopped on the far side of the weed patch and shouted for his mother. When she came out to see what the boy wanted, Ernie asked her to come and get him. His mother told him to come on through the weeds by himself. After the experience Ernie had just had, he couldn't have crossed that patch of weeds if his life depended upon it!

After Ernie balked, however, his mother ordered him to come on through, and he began to cry. She told him if he didn't stop crying and come on through the weeds, she would spank him. Ernie couldn't stop crying, and he certainly couldn't walk through the weeds. The vision of the blue racer flooded his mind. So his mother came and got him, and she spanked him all the way back through the weeds. It was one of the two times, Ernie claimed, that his mother ever spanked him.

That evening when Ernie's father came in from the fields, his mother told him about the crazy boy who wouldn't walk through the weeds and had to be spanked. Ernie's father told her about the roses, the knife, and the snake.

Ernie's attempted gathering of the roses, he later claimed, had hurt his mother the most, and he heard her crying for a long time that night after she went to bed. She never forgot the incident. Even when Ernie had reached middle age and went back home to visit his family, sooner or later she would always say, "Do you remember the time I spanked you because you wouldn't walk through the weeds?" She would proceed to tell of the episode, not leaving out any of the details. Toward the end of the story, she always managed to get the hem of her apron up around her eyes, just in case she should need it, which, according to Ernie, she always did.

The Hugging Party and the Children's Hour

Bob Terrell said that his grandpa told him how stiff many of the mountain churches were in Western North Carolina in the late 1800s. "Walk in just about any of the white-painted churches at the forks of the country roads," he said, "or the small log churches in the backwoods, and you were bound to see segregation by sexes—the men sat on one side of the aisle, women on the other."

Grandpa said, "Hellfire and brimstone rained all over the congregations each Sunday morning. Leather-lunged preachers went about their jobs as if it were their sole responsibility to pump enough salvation into the members to at least get them through the coming week."

Grandpa claimed that the ministers and their deacons frowned on everything social, except all-day singings and dinner on the grounds. Bingo was the next thing to the unpardonable sin. Bob said that's why it was so surprising when he found a newspaper clipping that referred to an item published on January 10, 1902. It told about a "hugging party" sponsored by one of the area churches. The little church was in need of funds, and, searching for some ways to raise money, some of the women hit upon the idea of the hugging party.

According to the newspaper, those who organized the party set up a schedule of rates as follows:

Two-minute hug. . . . . fifteen cents
Fifteen-minute hug . . . . fifty cents
Hugging another man's wife. . . . . one dollar
Hugging an old maid, no time limit . . three cents

Approximately 500 people attended the hugging party, the story reported, and all the young folks had a great time. The deacons of the church, especially those with pretty wives, weren't sure they enjoyed the party so much.

The news item concluded: "The young ladies of the church want to give another social to completely clear the church debt, but the older members protest. The editor hopes, if another one is given, he can be present with at least three cents."

Meanwhile, on Sunday afternoons in a nearby church, the pastor sometimes presented to the younger people a program known as "The Children's Hour." He always looked forward to this time with the children, because he usually gained some valuable insight into human nature while teaching the young-sters some basic truths. The children openly responded to his talks, and, in turn, the pastor garnered material to help him "scratch where it really itches" when dealing with youngsters.

One service featured pictures drawn by the pastor with chalk, illustrating a message on the fruits of righteousness and unrighteousness. He drew a tree filled with all sorts of fruit, labeling each fruit and commenting upon whether it was desirable or undesirable. When he came to the fruit labeled "stealing," much emphasis was given to this particular evil.

The message was apparently getting through to the chil-dren well, for suddenly a little seven-year-old boy stood and shouted, "My daddy steals, but I never will!"

The pastor hastened on to the next fruit, hoping the father, who happened not to be in attendance, would not be advised of the disclosure by his young son. However, when the little boy came back to the evening service, accompanied by his mother and father, he was carrying a large cushion with him, and he carefully sat on it during the service.

Belial, the Razorback Hog

In 1913, Horace Kephart, the late explorer/hiker/journalist, wrote an account of some of his experiences in the Great Smoky Mountains. These notes have since become public domain, but far too few of the public are acquainted with his informative and delightful writings. That is why I take this opportunity to share with you this particular event in Kephart's encounters with nature.

"If you camp out in the mountains," Horace Kephart wrote, "nothing will molest you but razorback hogs." He claimed that bears would flee from the camper, and wildcats would silently sneak away to their dens. But, Kephart said, "The moment the incense of cooking arises from your camp, every pig within two miles will smell it and hasten to call. You may throw your arm out of joint waving them off; they will laugh in your face. You may even curse in five languages; it is music to their titillating ears." (This apparently means that everything attempted by Kephart to scare off the hogs seemed to do just the opposite. It seemed to excite them and attract them even more!)

Kephart admired the hogs even while detesting them. He claimed that when it came to courage and shrewdness, no other animal could match these pigs. In the words of Kephart, "The razorback has a mind of his own; not instinct, but mind—whatever psychologists may say. He thinks. He bears grudges, broods over indignities, and plans redresses for the morrow or the week after. If he cannot get even with you, he will lay [a trap] for your unsuspecting friend. . . .

"Throughout summer and autumn, I cooked out of doors on the woodsman's range of forked stakes and lug pole spanning parallel beds of rock. When the pigs came, I fed them red-pepper pie. After one taste, they all said good-bye to my hospitality, except for one slab-sided, tusky old boar—and he planned a campaign to get even with me. At the first smell of smoke each day he would start for my premises.

"Hiding securely in a nearby thicket, he would spy on the operations until my stove got to simmering gently and I would retire to the cabin and get my fists in the bread dough. Then, charging at full speed, he would knock down a stake, trip the lug pole, and send my dinner flying. Every day he would do this!

"It got so that I had to sit there facing the fire all through my cooking, or that beast of a hog would ruin me. With this, I thought he was out-generaled. Idle dream!

"He would slip off to my neighbor Bob's place, break through the garden fence, and raise a ruckus—all because he hated me for that peppery fraud. He knew that Bob and I were friends.

"I dubbed this pig Belial [demon], a name that Bob promptly adapted to his own notion by calling it Be-liar. 'That Be-liar,' Bob swore, 'would cross hell on a rotten rail ta git into my tater patch!'

"Finally, I could stand it no longer and took down my rifle. It was a nail-driver [highly accurate], and I, through constant practice, was in good form. However, in the mountains it is more heinous to kill another man's pig than to shoot the owner. So, not knowing for sure that Belial didn't belong to someone rather than being wild, I took craft for my guide and guile for my counsel.

"I stalked Belial as stealthily as ever any hunter crept on

an antelope against the wind. At last I had him dead right: broadside to me and motionless as if in a daydream. I knew if I drilled his ear or shot his tail clean off, it would only make him meaner than ever.

"Belial sported an uncommonly fine tail and was proud to flaunt it. So I drew down on that part of his anatomy, purposely a trifle scant, and fired. Away scuttled that boar, with a broken tail that would dangle and cling to him disgracefully through life.

"Exit Belial! It was equivalent to a broken heart. He emigrated, or committed suicide, I know not which, but the Smoky Mountains knew him no more!"

Robert's Story

Robert Hodges's story is almost identical to thousands of others told by older people around America who are about Robert's age. We need to hear such stories over and over again today. I'm sure you know people who can share similar experiences with you personally. I hope you will ask them to, before they're gone. This is Robert's story—and his father's.

"Every Father's Day, it all comes back to me," Robert said. "Daddy was born in 1901, here in Tennessee. At age fifty-four he was buried less than five miles from where he was born. He never knew anything but hard work. He went at it six days a week, every week, every month, every year, farming that land.

"We all pitched in when we could, but Daddy wanted to make sure we went to school and, in his words, 'got some schoolin'.' He never got past the sixth grade, but all of us kids went through high school. When the youngest graduated, I guess that was probably one of the proudest moments of Daddy's life.

"He was always working at something. If he wasn't plowing, planting, sowing, or harvesting, he was chopping wood, milking the cows, or killing and preparing the hogs for the smokehouse. With all this, he probably never made much more than a $1,000 a year during his life. But he kept the family fed, and we were happy. Daddy might have been the happiest of all. He loved working.

"Of course, we were poor, materially. But we didn't know it. We had as much as anybody else we knew. And the riches we had far outweighed the poverty we went through. As I said, though, we didn't realize we were living in poverty. I know it sure didn't affect the quality of our lives together.

"Most of the crops Daddy harvested went to pay for the family needs. Mama had a garden that mostly took care of what we ate. She was always canning things, storing up for winter and for when the crops weren't so good.

"Daddy was the oldest of the children in his family. Mama was the oldest in hers. Their brothers and sisters had left the area, moved to the city. During World War II, I remember that my aunts and uncles and their kids would come to see us a lot. I thought they got to take a lot of trips and vacations, something we never did.

"Later, however, I learned about the rationing that was going on during the war. My relatives, even though they had money, couldn't get what they needed. So—and I'm not trying to be mean when I say this—they were coming to sponge off Mama and Daddy.

"Mama and Daddy always took care of us kids first, though. Looking back now, I don't know how they did it, but we always celebrated our birthdays and always received presents of some kind. Not much, but we always got something.

"And Christmas. Christmas was big at our house. Each of the kids always received a toy gift, along with fruit and nuts. I still have vivid memories of a red wagon, a wooden scooter, and a cap pistol with a belt and holster, a few of the gifts I got through the years. Choosing, cutting, and decorating the Christmas tree was always an unbelievably great event.

"Daddy was strict. There's no doubt about that. But we knew he was strict. So we acted and talked accordingly. I can't recall ever hearing Daddy swear. For that matter, I don't recall ever hearing him say anything bad about anybody, either. And he didn't allow us to.

"Hard work, good values, loyalty, and self-reliance are the things that Daddy instilled in us. He didn't talk much. I can't recall his ever telling me that he loved me. He didn't have to. I knew he did. And he knew that I knew.

"Eventually, there were eight kids in our family—I was the first one, then came Rebecca. When we were just little things, I recall one time when Mama cleaned us up and stood on the porch with us, looking for Daddy to come home from a trip he'd taken into town to get some supplies. When she saw him, she told us to run and meet him. He picked up both of us in his arms and carried us back to the house. That's about the only time I can ever remember being in his arms.

"Sometimes, he would take me with him when he split firewood. If he had to go get something while he was working, he would point toward a block of wood and tell me to sit on it until he got back. I never left that piece of wood. When he returned, I would always be there, like I was glued to it.

"But I guess the thing that's branded in my mind the most about Daddy is how he helped me get started in what became a very good career for me.

"The Korean War had ended; I was discharged from the army and came home. That first night I was home, right after dinner, as we were sitting around talking, Daddy asked me what I was going to do now that the war was over and I was a civilian again.

"I told him that I thought I would just sort of rest up a little, draw the money the government said they would pay me for six months, and then decide what I wanted to do.

"He let me know in no uncertain terms that I wasn't going to sit around and draw money from the government! As a matter of fact, he made it clear to all us kids that none of us was to ever get paid for not working!

"Daddy helped me look around town for a job. In two days,

I began working at a hardware store. Eventually, this led to working for one of the store's distributors and to the regional sales manager job I had until I retired.

"My wife and I reared three kids of our own, and you better believe I often thought of what Daddy would do as I had to deal with the challenges of their growing up. I thanked him many times. I still do."

The Reverend Noah Maples

In the early 1900s, the Reverend Noah Maples held many revivals in the mountains, and he never knew exactly what conditions he would encounter at the various homes he was a guest in for a night or two.

Reverend Noah enjoyed hot black coffee to help get his day started, and he always carried a bag of coffee beans in his saddlebags. Before the woman of the house began preparing for breakfast, he would tell her that he sure would appreciate a cup of hot coffee. If she didn't have any on hand, his reply would be that he "just happened" to have some with him. Then he would give her the coffee beans to grind and prepare for his favorite drink.

One morning, he gave a kind woman some coffee, then he and the husband went outside to do a few chores and then sit and talk as the wife prepared breakfast. After what was a much longer than usual wait, the husband excused himself and went in to see what was taking so long. He was back in a short time, apparently satisfied with the preparation progress, telling the reverend that everything was done except for the coffee, "and it ain't hardly tender yet."

Reverend Nash looked at the man in a strange sort of way, wondering, "*Tender* coffee?" When the reverend finally went into the kitchen to see this particular pot of coffee, he found the woman of the house testing it with a fork! Closer investigation revealed that instead of grinding the coffee beans, she had placed them in a pan, covered them with water, and added pork rind for flavoring!

The reverend also had some unusual experiences in the church buildings. At a revival meeting one evening, he had delivered an inspiring, soul-searching message, sharing with his hearers the question asked by Christ in the Sermon on the Mount: "Ye are the salt of the earth: but if the salt have lost his savour, wherewith shall it be salted?" Then Reverend Noah made an earnest appeal for consistency in living the Christian life, serving others, and openly sharing the Gospel. In closing, he gave the congregation an opportunity to quote their favorite Bible verses or to express in some way their appreciation of the message presented during the meeting.

The reaction was just what he had hoped and prayed for. The spirit of unconditional love and impregnable joy seemed to hover among everyone in attendance. It began when Sister Ogle stood and shared her testimony. Everyone knew it was genuine, for she was the epitome of one who lived daily with the Lord, regardless of her trials and tribulations. Sister Ogle's sons were present, and they were greatly moved by her words, knowing the testimony was real and realizing that they needed to get closer to the Lord by rededicating their lives to Him. Their actions resulted in other positive results from the congregation.

Just as everything seemed to be climaxing for a wonderful ending to an outstanding church experience, up jumped old Sidney Callahan, who had been half asleep during most of the service. Callahan had never been known for his intelligence nor for his faithful Christian service. And, unbeknown to Reverend Noah, Callahan's rising gave warning to others in the congregation that they were about to hear something entirely different.

Clearing his throat and shifting his chew of natural leaf from east to west and back again, Callahan drew himself up straight and wheezed out, "Reverend, I been a-settin' hyar a-listnin' to what ya had ter say, an I jes' 'bout decided that the bes' I can do fer yore proposition is ter say that I, too, have los' my Saviour, but I always been able to find Him whenever I gits back to whar I los' Him at."

Having cleared his system of his feelings on the matter, old Callahan took his seat, again shifted his chew, and closed his eyes in reverential awe. The benediction was hastily pronounced, and Reverend Noah retreated to solitude to recoup his spiritual and mental forces for the next meeting, longing for a cup of hot, black coffee.

In a revival meeting a few weeks later, an incident occurred that caused Reverend Noah to discontinue his practice of ending his services by asking the congregation to recite their favorite Bible verses.

His decision to discontinue the practice came the evening when long, lanky, elderly Frederick Whaley, with his drooping handlebar moustache, slowly arose from his seat, where he had been slumped down for peaceful rest during the past hour or so. He placed his lean, bony hands on the back of the pew in front of him, let his head fall between his arched shoulders, squinted his dark, eagle-like eyes at the reverend, and delivered with authority his favorite Bible verse: "Every tub must stand on its own bottom." Then he resumed his seat.

Having let the testimony from Sidney Callahan destroy an earlier meeting, Reverend Noah tried to nip this service-ending proclamation in the bud, while still wanting to give encouragement to this willing but uninformed man.

"Well, Brother Whaley," Reverend Noah said, "the truth carried in your verse is altogether valid. Personal responsibility is a very important matter. Every individual must give account of his own influence and must fight his own battles.

However, my dear brother, the verse you quoted, as great as it is, is not found in the Bible."

Not to be easily downed, Frederick Whaley, observing all the eyes turned on him, immediately arose and declared, "It's in my Bible all right."

Reverend Noah looked at Frederick, the congregation, and then back at Frederick. He wanted to get at the truth, but he also hated to embarrass Old Man Whaley. "That raises a serious question that must be settled," he said. "You and I, Brother Whaley, must be using different translations of the Bible." That's when Whaley informed the reverend that if he would accompany him home after the meeting, he would be glad to show him the verse in question.

People talked about that verbal encounter for years. They also talked about how they would pass by Frederick Whaley's cabin long after that evening and see him sitting on the porch, still diligently searching the Scriptures for the foundation of his statement with reference to the tub and its duty to rest upon its own bottom.

Reverend Noah Maples ceased asking for favorite Bible verses in his meetings.

More Than Tolerable

In 1918, ten-year-old Bud, his younger brother, and his two sisters were outside playing when the traveling peddler drove up the road in front of their house and stopped his wagon. For many isolated mountain families, the peddler represented the only opportunity to buy food and dry goods without having to go long distances into Gatlinburg or Sevierville.

The peddler was far more than a merchant on wheels, however. He also brought the latest news along with his goods, and he was often invited to eat with families along his route. That day, Bud's mother was in her straight-back chair on the front porch, peeling potatoes and watching her children play.

The peddler had always yelled happily to the children as he had approached the house on his previous trips. That day, however, Bud thought the man was acting strange. He didn't say hello to the children, didn't even tip his hat to their mother, as he usually did. He just drove up, stopped, took off his hat, and sat there in the wagon.

Bud knew something was wrong. His mother did, too. Bud watched her put down the potatoes and walk slowly to the wagon. Bud started to accompany her, but she told him to stay with his brother and sisters. He said that his mother just stood at the wagon for a few moments, talking with the peddler. Then, in Bud's words, "She just sort of went limp." The peddler gave her some candy for the children, put his hat back on, said something else to her, and then drove off. "Ma just stood there in the road for a while," Bud said. Finally, she brought the candy over to Bud and told him to share it with the other children.

"What's wrong, Ma?" Bud asked.

"Nothing," she replied as she bit her lip. She looked at the other children. They were anxious to get their rare candy treats. "Give it to 'em," she instructed Bud.

Bud knew how much his mother liked peppermint sticks. "Don't you want some?" he asked.

She shook her head, "No, son."

Bud knew something was terribly wrong. She almost never called him son. It was always Bud.

Supper that evening was sparse and quiet. After his mother got all the children to bed, Bud heard her crying herself to sleep. It wasn't until the next day, after she'd had time to think about it and pray about it, that she told Bud and the others that their father had been killed in the war. Bud said that's when he had to leave school for good, to work full time so he could help take care of the family. Three years later, his mother died.

"I just didn't know what to do the day Ma died," Bud recalled. "I remember going up under the pines in the hills. I lay down in the soft warm needles and cried myself to sleep. When I woke up, I cried some more. Then I prayed. I really didn't know how to pray, but I just talked to God, asking Him to help me to understand and to help me to do what needed to be done now that everything was on my shoulders. Only with God's help could I raise my brother and sisters like Ma and Pa would want me to."

Many years later, when Bud told this story, he could still recall the day his mother was buried.

"They put Ma in the back of a wagon and hauled her up to the graveyard. They couldn't get the wagon all the way up the hill, so the neighbors carried her up the rest of the way to the burying ground. I remember holding the hands of my two sisters as my brother held on to my coat. I also remember thinking how that was the longest hill I'd ever climbed.

"I could smell the flowers for Ma's grave. She always liked flowers. She was a simple woman. It didn't take much to make her happy. She was content with just the feel of her kids' arms around her neck. She liked to feel the softness of her feed-sack apron. Ma was like that.

"When I heard the preacher at her funeral talk about the fine mansions in heaven and how one had been prepared for Ma, I just couldn't picture her in a mansion. I thought about how she wouldn't like that, what with the folks being so fussy and all. I was thinking if she just had a little cabin, so long as it was neat and clean like she always kept our place, she would be happy.

"Then when the folks started singing 'Shall We Gather at the River,' I thought about how Ma didn't like rivers. They always scared her. She used to tell us kids to stay away from the river. I couldn't help wondering if there would be someone to help her across. She'd hate to have to tackle it by herself.

"I thought about things like that all through the funeral. My thoughts just got me lost I guess, because the next thing I remember was hearing everybody saying 'Amen.' Then we went back down the hill to the wagon.

"The house just wouldn't be the same, I thought, when we got home. Then I got to thinking that if we'd continue to talk to her just like she was there, it would ease the pain. So we just started setting Ma's plate at one end of the table and Pa's at the other end.

"Us kids would sit two on a side, talking to each other across the table and to Ma and Pa at the ends as we ate. If anyone would have heard us, they would have thought we were crazy or something. It helped, though, talking to our Ma and Pa just like they were there.

"A lot of times when I had decisions to make in dealing

with my brother and sisters and other people, I'd often talk that over with Ma and Pa, too, when nobody else was around.

"I reckon I got some pretty good advice from somewhere, from Ma, Pa, and God, because God was good to us, and we had a lot of blessings as the years passed by. My two sisters and my brother were healthy. They grew up, married, and moved away. All but me. I stayed in the Smokies. And life here has been more than tolerable."

The Pi Beta Phi Settlement School

In the early part of the twentieth century, there were quite a number of "college settlements" in our country. These settlements, usually sponsored and maintained by our larger universities, were commonly found in the tenement districts of major cities. Through the settlements, social work was carried out. The work consisted of assisting the less-fortunate and uneducated youth and adults. The settlements were there to help these people learn to read and write and to increase their capacity to enjoy life.

In the early 1900s, the nation's newspapers and magazines suddenly "discovered" the primitive life of people in the impoverished areas of the South. Written accounts informed the public that these people were actually living in "another world" deeply rooted in the past. The nation was moved by the descriptions of these backwoods people.

Pi Beta Phi, the first national college sorority organization for women, decided to do something about it. In 1910, Pi Beta Phi chose to establish a settlement school in a poverty-stricken area of the South. They asked the commissioner of education in Washington, D.C., to tell them where such a school was most needed. He sent Pi Beta Phi to Tennessee, where they met with the state board of education. The state board informed the group that Sevier County had fewer schools than any other county in the state at that time.

Continuing their pursuit, Pi Beta Phi representatives went to talk with the Sevier County school superintendent in Sevierville. He told the group that the people in and around Gatlinburg were in dire need of a school. He suggested an educational emphasis on industrial and agricultural subjects. "These mountain people don't want to leave," he said, "so they need training to help them earn a better living where they are."

The Pi Beta Phi settlement school opened in Gatlinburg in 1912. The teachers were initially shocked at how isolated from the rest of the world the children were. Nestled at the bottom of Mount LeConte, the third highest peak in the Great Smoky Mountains at 6,593 feet, Gatlinburg was shut in by the rugged mountains on every side and separated from the rest of society by almost impassable roads. The effects were apparent.

Approximately 200 families lived in and around Gatlinburg, most of them occupying mountainside cabins. The town itself consisted of only six or seven houses, three general stores, a blacksmith shop, and a Baptist church. Across from the church, Pi Beta Phi set up their school in a tiny shack they rented for $1.50 per month.

Before the arrival of Pi Beta Phi, Gatlinburg did have a school, but it was pitiful at best. The teachers, for the most part, were unqualified, and attendance was irregular. Thus, it couldn't be considered strange that in the beginning only thirteen children came, off and on, to the Pi Beta Phi school. The people of Gatlinburg were proud. They didn't want Pi Beta Phi to force a change upon them. They didn't want outside interference. Yet, deep down, these mountain people did want the educational opportunities the outsiders talked about offering to their children.

No miracles suddenly happened. Pi Beta Phi struggled to gain the support of the adults and the interest of other children. They asked parents to help them get children to come to school on a regular basis. They attempted to make learning for their students as exciting and as much fun as possible.

The school's facilities were poor, and the atmosphere of the dilapidated schoolhouse was depressing. Pi Beta Phi requested that the townspeople work with them in obtaining a new building. The request fell on deaf ears. Yet, Pi Beta Phi had grown to love these mountain people, and they wanted to acquire land to establish a permanent school for them. Still, the people rebelled against giving in to the outsiders. Discouragement eventually persuaded Pi Beta Phi that maybe the best thing to do would be to pack up and leave.

Pi Beta Phi eventually issued an ultimatum: "The people must do their part in buying land and showing they want our school. Otherwise, we will have to close it and leave." Pi Beta Phi pledged that they would contribute $600 toward the purchase of a seventy-acre tract of land on which to construct the settlement school. Pi Beta Phi told local storeowner, postmaster, and landowner Ephraim Ogle they would buy the land from him at the price of $1800. They weren't even certain he would sell, but they told him he would if he wanted the settlement school in Gatlinburg. A final hour was set, at which time the school would be moved to another community if the townspeople did not come through with the needed money.

That's when the handful of residents who had been longing for the school took a stand and made a last desperate struggle to obtain the land and keep Pi Beta Phi in Gatlinburg. The Pi Beta Phi teachers and administrators were already resigned to the fact that they were going to leave. No one had contributed any money, and Ephraim Ogle had not yet said he would sell, even if the money came in.

The teachers had their bags packed and were sitting on the porch of their cottage, waiting for the horse-drawn carriage to come and take them away. However, Mrs. Andy Huff and a few other supporters of the school were not going to give up.

Almost in hysteria, Mrs. Huff pulled her husband away from the logging camp he owned in the mountains and pleaded with him not to let the school get away. Andy Huff had been a booster from the outset, having personally taken his small daughter to school each day to encourage others to do likewise.

Andy Huff chipped in $250. Steve Whaley, another local businessman, quickly matched the $250. They were still short $700, even if Ephraim Ogle decided to sell. Meanwhile, the carriage for the teachers was headed toward their cottage. Excitement was high when Ephraim Ogle walked over to the teacher's cottage, ahead of the carriage, and said he was willing to sell. He also said he would contribute $250 toward the purchase price. Andy Huff and businessman Isaac Maples promised they would take care of the final $450. The carriage left Gatlinburg without its passengers, and the Pi Beta Phi Settlement School was in Gatlinburg to stay!

But the story doesn't end here. Not only did the children benefit from Pi Beta Phi's presence, but the adults gained tremendous benefits as well. Rel Maples, born in 1905 and the founder of the renowned Gatlinburg Inn, claimed that the Pi Beta Phi Arrowmont School of Arts and Crafts did more for Gatlinburg than the establishment of the Great Smoky Mountains National Park. Son of David Crockett Maples, Jr. (a postman on horseback for thirty-three years) and maternal grandson of Ephraim Ogle, Rel said that Pi Beta Phi furnished women the thread with which to weave, worked with them, and marketed their finished products. They also assisted the men with materials and techniques, and marketed their subsequent wood-carved products. This leadership established income for the families and exposed their beautiful handiwork—and the area—throughout the United States.

The Mother's Day Gifts

Mother's Day was coming up. Robert and his brother, John, had never given their mother a gift on this special occasion before, but this time they made up their minds they were going to do it. They figured they were old enough—Robert was ten and John was eight—and besides, they recently had become lucky. Through their dad, a carpenter, they were introduced to the man who owned the new hotel in town, and this man said they could hang around the lobby and carry people's suitcases. He paid each boy a nickel per week, and they got to keep all the tips they received.

This would be the boys' first "real" gift to their mother. On her birthday and Christmas, their dad always made sure to get her something and tell her it was from all of them. At times, the boys had picked her some flowers for her birthday or had found some pretty pinecones or river rocks or something for her Christmas gift, but the "real" store-bought gifts were always chosen and paid for by their dad. This time it was going to be different.

Things were pretty rough in their Smoky Mountain community in the early 1930s, and money was hard to come by. Even though the boys had not made much money from their new job, they had already learned how to make the most of the little they had. The boys told their dad of their plan, and he assured them their mother would be very happy over their decision. When Mother's Day neared, the boys divided up the money they had earned, deciding to individually choose and pay for two different gifts.

Robert had been thinking for a long time about the gift he wanted to give his mother. He knew that she would like to wear one of those shiny pins on her dress at church, like some of the other women wore. He had seen her admire the pins, and he had heard her mention how pretty they were. He also remembered how she said she might save some money someday and get one. They had some of these pins in one of the racks at the general store, and Robert calculated that he had just enough money to buy one.

Robert didn't tell John about the gift. He wanted it to be a surprise to everyone. Of course, John decided to keep his gift a secret also. Even their dad, with all of his persuasive power, could not get either boy to reveal what each had purchased. Everyone in the family seemed to enjoy the secrecy. Their mother had no idea she was going to receive any gifts, and their father had no idea what the gifts might be. The brothers spent a lot of time trying to guess what each other had bought, but there was no way either was going to tell.

Mother's Day arrived. The family had finished breakfast and were dressed for church when the boys decided to spring the surprise. From behind their backs they brought forth packages wrapped in tissue paper, Robert's tied with twine and John's twisted tightly to make the paper cling to the gift it concealed. Their mother, to say the least, was very surprised. Mother's Day, after all, still was a relatively new observance.

"You can open John's first, Mom," Robert suggested. John responded to this with a face-widening grin, anxious for his mother to tear away the paper from his gift to her. Her face was aglow as she carefully untwisted the tissue. Sunlight coming through the open window bounced off the shiny object being released from the wrapping. Their mother glowed more than ever as she took the pin from the paper and held it to her dress.

"Oh, John," she said softly, with a mist in her eyes, "it's beautiful."

John beamed. Robert's jaw dropped and his heart sank. It was just like the pin he had bought for her—a shiny flower on a stem with two leaves. Before Robert had time to speak or react further, however, his mother was unwrapping his gift, glowing twice as much as she attached it to her dress, opposite John's pin.

"These are perfect," she said, again with mist in her eyes. She studied their faces, John's still beaming and Robert's now beginning to break into a smile. "I don't know how you two knew exactly what I wanted—matching pins!" The boys looked at one another and grinned, while their mother slipped a wink to their dad. She wore the pins every Sunday to church—the only lady in the entire community with matching flower pins!

Miss Emmie and the Edison Graphophone

A couple of other stories in this collection pertain to Lena Penland Purkey, who was born in 1904 in Slabtown, Tennessee, and at an early age moved from her Cocke County residence to a farm near Hot Springs, North Carolina. Sometimes, when all the chores around the house and farm were done, Lena's mother would take all the younger children and go visiting. They especially liked to visit Miss Emmie, who lived up the creek from them. Miss Emmie had married late in life, and she and her husband, Lum, had no children. According to Lena, Miss Emmie loved the young people of the community and always welcomed them to her home.

Miss Emmie and Lum lived in a large, sturdy log house Miss Emmie's father had built when he first came into this remote settlement as chief landowner. The hand-hewn logs had long since been covered with weatherboard, and there was a long front porch extending the length of the house, well-covered by a network of honeysuckle vines.

On the porch, Lena said, Miss Emmie often brought the children delicious tidbits from her kitchen, such as hot, butter-filled biscuits that melted in their mouths and pans full of crisp cracklins or toasted pork rinds fresh from the oven.

Lena remembered her as a good neighbor who had many

admirable traits, but Miss Emmie still clung to many of the old superstitions handed down from her ancestors. She was convinced, for example, that a fifty-cent piece dropped into the churn would cause the butter to "gather." Lena didn't believe in such superstitions, but as she grew older, she did begin to notice how much money Miss Emmie was able to collect from her husband, Lum!

On winter days, Lena said all the children liked to bask in front of Miss Emmie's fireplace, which held a special charm all its own. The face of the fireplace was plastered with white clay she had taken from the creek bank. The hearth was made of large, smooth, flat stones. The two tall, slender dog irons had been forged by her father long ago. The old clock ticking pleasantly on the mantel had also belonged to her parents. Lena said that the wide-plank floor of Miss Emmie's front room was covered with a variegated carpet she had woven on her own loom. A big pink conch shell and other interesting curiosities lay on the tall bureau by the window.

On one visit, Miss Emmie opened the bureau drawers and showed Lena, her mother, and the other children the contents. She presented a large roll of Confederate money which had belonged to her father, along with many tintype pictures of her kinfolk. A long lock of iron gray hair belonging to Miss Emmie's mother impressed young Lena the most. Holding it up for all to see, Miss Emmie claimed, "I believe it grows a little bit every year."

To Lena, the hall bedroom between the front room and the kitchen was fascinating, too. There, Miss Emmie kept her spinning wheel, her tallest feather bed, with fat pillows covered by stiffly starched pillow shams, her round-top trunk, and a large dusting broom made of peacock feathers. "How we children admired the long, colorful feathers," Lena said. "It was a joy to touch them." Lena smiled slightly and got a faraway look in her eyes as she said, "Yes, Miss Emmie saw beauty in the simplest things. This beauty was reflected in all the interesting odds and ends she had collected and displayed throughout her house."

In warm weather, the children enjoyed playing in Miss Emmie's cool backyard, where lilacs, snowballs, and sweet-smelling shrubs grew. Old bricks encircled a pansy bed, and a boxwood grew so tall that Lena said the chickens used it for a roosting place. A gnarled old cedar towering over one end of the house gave pleasant shade and protection. The entire house and yard were enclosed by a picket fence, with a swinging gate at each of the two entrances.

Across the road in front of the house sat the blacksmith shop where Miss Emmie's husband, Lum, shoed the neighborhood horses. Occasionally, he would let Lena and the other children pump the bellows that fanned the coals into flame, or let them stand at a safe distance to watch while a horse was being shod.

"Any home that owned any sort of musical instrument was a popular gathering place for the youngsters," Lena said. "A few families in the cove had organs, and one family had a piano—but the biggest attraction of all was the Edison Graphophone. A neighbor living a mile or so down the creek bought one, along with thirty cylinder records." Lena's brothers Hubert and Willie were the first members of her family to see and hear this "talking machine."

Lena was on edge with curiosity after hearing her brothers tell about the big blue and white "morning glory" horn. They told her that you could put on a record, crank up the machine, and the music came out of the horn. She said that her brothers went around the house singing snatches from "Uncle Josh" and "The Preacher and the Bear" with an air of superiority. Lena was determined to see and hear this world-shaking wonder for herself. She bided her time as patiently as she could. Luckily, she didn't have to wait too long.

"Wes and I were sent on an errand that took us right by the house of the owner of this magic instrument. It was a hot summer day and the road was dusty. On pretense of wanting a drink of water, we stopped by. We were asked to sit and rest awhile, as was the custom of mountain people. We sat.

"Finally, we were asked if we would like to hear 'Uncle Josh' on the talking machine. Indeed we would! The music was heavenly. We peered long and searchingly into the big morning glory horn, half expecting to see Uncle Josh step out." Lena and her brother Wes had stopped, supposedly, to get a drink of water, but they never budged from their chairs until they had heard all thirty of the Graphophone records.

Pills, Antiseptics, and Soft Prayers

Shortly before he died, it was my privilege to hear Dr. Robert Thomas tell of some of his experiences as a medical missionary in the Great Smoky Mountains area. In 1926, when Dr. Thomas arrived at Pittman Center, a settlement about twelve miles from Gatlinburg, he felt as if he had stepped back into a period of history long past.

Even though the people of Pittman Center were not far from Gatlinburg or Sevierville and not too removed from Knoxville, they were not actually a part of the same world. In their dress, their customs, and beliefs, the inhabitants of one of the last frontiers in America were almost untouched by outside influences. Indoor toilet facilities were unheard of, and no one had a lavatory.

Everyone still washed, drank, and cooked with water drawn from a well or stream. Windows had no screens on them, and, of course, telephones and radios were nonexistent. These people had no need for books or newspapers, since most of the residents could neither read nor write. Ten, twelve, or even fourteen members of a family would share one room, sleeping in three or four beds.

The people of Pittman Center were superstitious. They believed in the existence of witches and all sorts of evil powers. Dr. Thomas discovered they killed witches by drawing pictures of them and making large hearts on the pictures. Then, taking a picture out into the woods to a secret place, they would fasten it to a tree by driving a knife through the heart. This action, they believed, along with refusing to associate with the witches in any way, would cause the witches to grow sick and lose their powers.

Prior to Dr. Thomas's arrival, the people did all of their own doctoring. "Granny women" carried the main medical duties. Herbs, poultices, potions, and roots were combined with righteousness and rituals to cure anything that might come along. However, Dr. Thomas found people suffering from tuberculosis, contagious eye diseases, chronic diarrhea, parasitic worms, typhoid, diphtheria, smallpox, and other communicable diseases. Dr. Thomas came across people— sometimes entire families—suffering from pellagra. This dietary condition leads to habitual depression and melancholia. These people lost their appetites and energy.

It wasn't easy for Dr. Thomas when he entered their world. They "suspicioned a furriner" carrying a black bag full of black magic evils. When asked to choose between a disease or a vaccination, disease seemed the lesser of two evils. The people preferred to stick with the ways of the "granny women," even though family graveyards attested to the fact that relatively few people got well after becoming sick. Crudely carved inscriptions on tombstones often read: "12 yeers; 1 yeer; 10 daze."

For typhoid, one homemade treatment was a pan of water placed under the sick person's bed to stop the fever. Boiled and sweetened sheep dung was a sure cure for measles. Spider webs were placed on cuts and other raw wounds. For childbirth, it was believed that labor pains would be eased if the husband would sink an ax into the floor under the bed on which his wife was giving birth.

Dr. Thomas did his best as he fell in love with these people, and he gave his life ministering to their needs. He went among them day in and day out, riding horseback up and down the hills, carrying saddlebags full of medicines people could accept or refuse.

As the years became decades and Dr. Thomas ceased being a "furriner," few people continued to reject what he had to offer. They began to trust him and began to grow healthier as a result. Dr. Thomas told of a visit he had in a home several years after his arrival in the area. The family summoned him, an act of progress in itself.

On this dreary, sticky night, rain beat upon the house and, in spots, dripped through the ceiling. Dr. Thomas was called to a bed where a young man lay extremely ill. The large family stood silent in the shadows as he examined the boy by the light of a dim, flickering candle. Symptoms of dizziness and poor coordination led the doctor to suspect the young man had a brain tumor and would have to be taken to Knoxville for surgery.

Dr. Thomas was stuck with the problem of telling the parents of his diagnosis, not knowing how they would accept it, not knowing even if they would accept it. He looked at the mother, a devout Christian lady, and at the father, a man who wasn't known for his kindness and compassion.

"We ought to realize what kind of situation the boy is in," Dr. Thomas said in his explanation to the couple, "and we ought to pray." His words appeared to help. The parents began to face their problem with poise. They trusted Dr. Thomas and allowed him to take their son to Knoxville, where he could get care that could not be supplied any longer by the local "granny women."

As one speaker later declared at a banquet honoring Dr. Thomas, "The special genius of Dr. Robert F. Thomas was that he entered into the fundamentalist world of the Great Smoky Mountains and respected it, but insisted upon ministering to its true needs. An evangelist performing only histrionically to the emotions of the people would have been great on a Sunday but forgotten on a Monday. Dr. Thomas was the man who was there every day, with pills, antiseptics, and soft prayers."

The Walker Sisters

The Walker sisters were living legends in the Great Smoky Mountains. The family of John and Margaret Walker, who married in 1866, included eleven children, but five of the sisters—Louisa, Margaret, Martha, Hettie, and Polly—refused to move from their log home when the Great Smoky Mountains National Park was established in 1934. Even though their home was in the park boundaries, the National Park Service agreed to let them remain as long as they lived. The government paid them for the property and put the money in a Knoxville bank for them.

The Walker sisters were one of the Smokies' major attractions. After receiving international attention in a featured article in the *Saturday Evening Post,* tourists came from all over to see these wonders of the world, who lived in the twentieth century in a nineteenth-century fashion. They had no electricity, cut their own wood for the fireplace and cookstove, planted a garden for all of their vegetables, tended sheep, carded wool, and made clothing and bedding on looms. They ground their own meal from corn. Eventually, their mule lost most of his teeth, so they also had to grind corn for him.

"In his old age," Margaret once said, "that mule's got so bullheaded he won't let us girls work him anymore. When we want the land plowed or the logs dragged down from the mountain for firewood, one of our relatives has to come and work him for us. An old Tennessee mule has got to be handled special, and none of us cuss."

The sisters fought off bears that ripped up their garden. They chased foxes, weasels, and hawks that killed their chickens. They were constantly on the lookout for menacing razorback hogs. Their garden not only grew staple vegetables, but had rows of flowers separating ordinary vegetables such as corn and turnips from the mint, horehound, horseradish, parsley, and sage. The sisters were noted for their prize orchard, which included apple, chestnut, peach, plum, and cherry trees. They put bells on their turkeys so hunters would not mistake them for wild turkeys. They had names for all their animals, including their sheep.

Once, a photographer wanted to get a picture of the sisters shearing sheep, so Margaret called out to them, "Here, sheepie, sheepie, sheepie!" The sheep came. As they were approaching, they suddenly bolted back up the mountain. Margaret explained, "They won't come back down again as long as there is anybody around with pants on."

John Walker had been a loving but strict father prior to his death in 1921. If males called on the girls, they had to leave when he went to bed. He always retired at sundown, and the girls had to do the same. Margaret once said, "Pa never held with parties and such frivolities, so we never went to many. We did attend a few apple peelin's and a corn huskin' or two."

Aware of their strict upbringing and beliefs, a tourist asked the sisters if they thought heaven would condone dancing.

One sister replied, "You can risk it if you want to, but don't do it here."

When a visitor once asked Margaret if he could smoke in her presence, she replied, "It'll only make two people sick, you and me."

The sisters' mother, Margaret King Walker, was an exceptional woman, and they drew much of their strength and resolve from her. All eleven of her children lived to become adults, a feat in itself in those days. Margaret King Walker died in 1909, at age sixty-two.

The time Mrs. Walker found a weasel in her chicken house is one remarkable episode from her life. Hearing a commotion, she went out to inspect the chicken house and discovered a weasel with one of the chickens. When she reached to get the chicken, the weasel bit into her hand, refusing to let go. Mrs. Walker calmly walked over and stuck her hand and the weasel into a water barrel. The weasel drowned in the blood-stained water. Her comment? "I knew sooner or later it'd turn loose."

The John Walker family never had an outdoor toilet like other families of the era. Mrs. Walker wouldn't have one because of the odor it would cause. So, from the very beginning, the females always used the woods far below the house, and the males used the woods far above the house.

Besides the five famous sisters, the Walker family had one more girl. Carolina Walker married J. P. Shelton and left the old homeplace. She died in 1966, at age eighty-two.

Many people wondered why none of the other Walker sisters ever married. Interviewed in 1946, J. P. Shelton had his own idea of why. "Reckon I'm about the only man that had courage to bust into that family," he said. "Or else, the rest of them girls got discouraged when they couldn't get me and jus' quit."

The truth of the matter is, however, that Martha was engaged to a man named John Daniels, and Polly was engaged to a logger by the name of Cotter. Both fiancées met with accidental deaths. Polly took the death of her fiancée so badly that she became extremely ill and never fully recovered.

The Walkers' 150-year-old log home still remains. Even though the creation of the Great Smoky Mountains National Park preserved some of the most magnificent land in the world, the Walker Sisters never did appreciate the government interference. Louisa was the poet for the sisters, and when they were forced to sell their land, even though they could remain on it, the fun-loving, brown-eyed woman, who had a perpetual smile, penned these nostalgic lines: "But now the park commissioner / Comes all dressed in clothes so gay / Saying this old mountain home of yours / We must take away."

Of the five famed Walker sisters who made time stand still, Polly was the first to go. She died when she was sixty-nine, in 1945. Hettie left them in 1947 at age fifty-eight. Martha passed away in 1951 at the age of seventy-four. Margaret, at age ninety-two, preceded Louisa in death in 1962. Louisa, the last, died in 1964 at the age of eighty-two. Interviewed just prior to her death, Louisa said that her mother and father left the children a love for God and a love of home and family, along with an appreciation of good hard work. "Pa loved to work," Louisa said, "and Ma, well, she just loved life and everything about it."

Mountain Hospitality

In the early 1900s, travelers who journeyed to the Great Smoky Mountains to take in the scenery, unspoiled forests, and good fishing found accommodations to be extremely primitive. The good hotels at the summer resorts were few and far between. Many of the inns were dirty, and much of the food would cause one to consider fasting. It was said that the best method of staying in the mountains during those days was for the travelers to take their own food and tents and camp out. That way they could be assured of edible meals and a clean place to stay. Far in the backcountry, however, the mountaineers usually opened their humble homes to all travelers.

The hospitality of these Smoky Mountain inhabitants knew no bounds. Unless there was sickness in the family or they were just so destitute they didn't have anything to share, they treated traveling strangers like one of the family. Such an open-door policy accounts for the fact that travelers often imposed upon poor people without realizing it. Later, these same guests might even criticize the scanty fare, when they may have been given a lion's share of the last bit of food in the house.

One traveler during this period tells of how he was trying to find a shortcut through the forest and became lost. In his words, "Sunset found me on the summit of an unfamiliar mountain, with cold rain setting in. . . . I turned back to the head of the nearest watercourse, not knowing where it led, and fought my way through thicket and darkness to the nearest house and asked for lodging. The man was just coming in from work. He showed some anxiety, but admitted me with solemn politeness. Then he departed on an errand, leaving his wife to hear the story of my wanderings.

"I was eager for supper, but the woman of the house made no move toward the kitchen. An hour passed. The smallest child in this rather large family whimpered with hunger. The mother, flushing in my presence, soothed the baby with milk from her breast.

"It was well on in the night when her husband returned, bearing a little poke of cornmeal. Then the woman flew to her woodstove. Soon, we had hot bread, three or four slices of pork, along with unsweetened black coffee.

"I later discovered that upon my arrival there had barely been enough cornmeal for the family's supper and breakfast. Without my knowing it, my host had to shell some corn, go in almost pitch darkness, without a lantern, to a tub mill down the stream, wait while it ground out a few spoonfuls per minute, and then bring the meal back.

"Next morning when I offered to pay, the kindly mountaineer waved it aside, saying, 'I ain't never took money from company, and this ain't no time to begin.'

"Smiling, and with a tear in my eye, I slipped some coins into the hand of the eldest child. 'This is not pay,' I said, 'it's a present.'

"The young girl to whom I gave the coins was awed into speechlessness at the sight of money of her own. The parents did not know how to thank me for her, but said, 'Stay on, stranger. Poor folk has a poor way, but you're welcome to what we'uns got.'"

Not long ago the custom of opening homes to travelers was still common in the Great Smoky Mountains area. Before hotels and motels sprang up in abundance, it wasn't unusual for a man to come home from work and discover that his wife had invited a family of tourists to spend the night. One elderly minister friend of mine said that he and his wife often picked up extra money in the early days by renting out their bedroom and sleeping on the living room sofa. "But sometimes," he said, "my wife would get carried away."

Then the elderly minister chuckled to himself, remembering, "One night I came home from preaching a revival. It was late, and not wanting to awaken my wife, I started tiptoeing to the bedroom in darkness. But then, I stumbled over a body, then another, then another. Finally, I turned on the light and discovered eighteen people camping out on my living room floor!"

The Right Decision

In the early 1930s, Paul Arnold and his wife struggled to make a right decision. Paul was the pastor of a backwoods church in the Smokies, and his congregation knew they had a jewel. The pastor seemed to be bound by no denominational lines as he delivered God's message to everyone, preaching about God's unconditional love and forgiveness. He painted his words in such a way that listeners were not only inspired, they were moved to action to make a positive difference in their lives and the lives of others. Pastor Arnold brought to life the Ten Commandments in a practical way and illustrated how the Sermon on the Mount was just as relevant in his day and time as when it was first presented to people in need of spiritual guidance.

One summer, a traveler from a large city happened to attend one of the pastor's services. As the mountain pastor spoke, he moved this visitor as no minister had ever done. Following the service, the city man was greeted at the front door by the pastor and spoke briefly with him. He found Paul Arnold to be just as insightful and caring out of the pulpit as he was in it.

About a year later, the city man's church lost their pastor. The man immediately thought of Paul Arnold. Pastor Arnold was contacted and invited to visit the city church and preach. When he spoke to that sophisticated group in his simple but powerful manner, they, like the visitor a year earlier, were deeply touched and extremely impressed. Before he returned to the mountains, Paul Arnold was asked to become pastor of the large church.

Paul was elated. On the way home, he thought of how he and his wife and children had barely been able to survive on his inadequate salary. Now, this well-paying position in this prestigious church would open doors and allow opportunities he never dreamed possible.

When Pastor Arnold arrived home and shared the news with his wife, she shed tears of unbelievable happiness. However, after getting over the initial reaction to the offer, they began to ask themselves, "Who's going to take care of Mrs. Turner when her husband mistreats her, and who's going to confront Mr. Turner and bring him to his senses? Who's going to be around to serve as mediator between the mountain people and the law? Who's going to laugh and cry with these people and help them celebrate the good times and ride through the bad? Who's going to marry and bury these people?"

I think you know the decision Reverend Paul Arnold and his wife made. They agreed that the city folks needed them far less than the mountain people did. The couple stayed on in the mountains until they died, continuing to live in material poverty and spiritual riches.

Courage

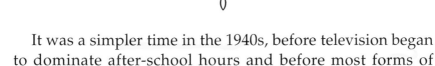

It was a simpler time in the 1940s, before television began to dominate after-school hours and before most forms of entertainment began to require electricity, batteries, or microchips.

Our story takes place during the spring and begins with a little girl who was glad to hear the school bell. After all, when you were six years old and lived in the Great Smoky Mountains, springtime was more fun outside than inside. As the little girl walked home from school, however, she thought about a word her teacher had used a few minutes earlier while reading a story to the class. The word was *courage,* and it sounded like such a good word the way the teacher had used it.

Soon, though, the word was pushed to the back of the girl's mind as she enjoyed the freshness of the air and the fragrance of things all around her coming to life after the harsh winter. Her mother had promised to take her for a stroll in the woods close to their house that afternoon. The little girl skipped the rest of the way home, throwing her books onto a chair as she entered the front door. She then gulped down a glass of milk before she and her mother began their excursion.

The mother and daughter talked about the budding trees and the daffodils rising up to show the potential of things to come. Then their talk gave way to silent appreciation as they soaked in the spring with all their senses.

Spring was interrupted, however, as they came to an area where the woods had been burned and the forest floor was black and barren. The damage apparently had occurred quite a while back, probably caused by campers who let a fire get out of control. The mother and daughter sat on a stump, taking the opportunity to rest and to imagine what had been there before the fire had erased all signs of life. That's when the word *courage* jumped to the front of the little girl's mind again, and some of the thoughts she had entertained previously were given new attention.

"What is courage?" she asked, looking up at her mother. "Is it like what our cat has when she sees a dog and lays her ears back and spits at him, even when he is ten times bigger than she is?"

The mother thought for a moment. "It's partly that," she replied, "but it's much more than that."

"Oh. . . ." the little girl responded, not really understanding what her mother meant. There was silence again before her mother shared her continuing thoughts.

"Remember how I've told you about Grandpa Willis and how he was a soldier in the war?"

The little girl nodded her head.

"Well, he told me about something that happened in that war—something that I think helps to define courage."

She began to relate a story about a young soldier during the bitter, bloody days of war in the muddy trenches of a foreign country. The soldier saw his friend fall in no-man's-land, that stretch of ground between his trench and the enemy's bastion. His friend lay in the mud, unable to move.

The young soldier asked his officer, "Sir, may I go and bring him back to our side?"

The officer denied the request, answering, "No one can live out there. The bullets are flying, and there's no place for you to hide. It's certain suicide. If you go, I will lose you as well."

The bonds of friendship were stronger than the compulsion

to obey, and the soldier dashed out to attempt to save his friend. They had been like brothers for many months. He made his way to the fallen young man, then knelt in the mud and grasped his buddy's limp body and slung him over his shoulders. Staggering under the load, he made his way back to their own trenches, only to fall mortally wounded with his friend.

The officer wept bitterly and almost shouted in anger to the dying young man, "I told you not to go. Now I've lost two good men. It wasn't worth it! It wasn't worth it!"

The young soldier looked up and, with a faint smile, said to his officer, "But it was worth it, sir. It was worth it, because when I got to him, before he died, he said, 'I knew you'd come.'"

The girl's mother finished her story and stood, reaching her hand down to grasp the hand of her daughter, who rose to meet her touch. "That is another part of courage," she told the wide-eyed girl.

Then the girl's mother saw something about ten yards from where they had been sitting. There, in the midst of the charred wood and burnt stubble, a yellow buttercup thrust itself up through the blackness. The mother pointed to the flower. "And that is courage," she said. With deep admiration, the mother and daughter looked at that yellow buttercup pushing up bravely through the burned-out forest floor.

Fair Fighting

Near the end of World War II, Sergeant Matt Wiley stepped off the train in his hometown in the foothills of the Smoky Mountains. Matt was beginning a well-earned thirty-day leave from his job as a tail gunner on a B-29 Superfortress.

When Matt exited the worn and frayed railroad coach, he expected to spend a relaxing month with his parents, who owned a small lumber business. Instead, he soon discovered that illness, despair, and potential financial ruin had beset his family. Matt's mother, who had not wanted to share the desperate situation with him in her letters, explained it to him a day after his return. His father was bedfast, suffering from a physical illness brought on by worry and day after day of intensive labor.

Matt's father faced the possibility of losing everything he had worked for years to establish. Mrs. Wiley told her son about a man named Parker who had bought a lumber mill nearby. Parker was unscrupulous. He had unfairly gained a number of wartime government contracts. He had sabotaged equipment at the Wiley Lumber Company. And everyone knew that Parker was behind some unexplained fires and labor strife at the Wiley family's business.

Mrs. Wiley told her son the local bank was holding a $12,000 note against them. She said her husband had a contract for a large order that would pay off the note. Parker, however, was blocking the completion of the job. If the note was not taken care of soon, all would be lost.

Having recently faced enemy planes from the tail of a B-29, Matt Wiley was not particularly afraid of Parker. He went to see him. In a calm, mild voice, Matt told him that the Wiley family certainly didn't mind fair competition. "As a matter of fact," he said, "Dad thrived upon such competition in the past."

Parker exploded. "If your father doesn't like the way I fight," he raged, "then it's his privilege to fight back the same way. I protect myself. If he has any backbone, let him do the same!"

Young Matt responded, "Dad can't fight your way. It's not a part of who he is. I know he would be defeated and lose everything he has rather than win unfairly. My father is a good man. He's always been fair and aboveboard. I'm proud of him for that." Matt left the meeting knowing he had to do what he had to do.

For a week, Matt used his military training to define and solve his family's situation. He studied maps of the woodlands surrounding the area. He spent hours in the musty basement of the courthouse, searching through old deeds. He sat on the well-worn public benches down at the town square, talking with boyhood friends who knew how the political winds of the county were blowing.

Gradually, Matt began to develop a plan. In a few more days, his strategy started to bear fruit as he visited county offices, showed maps and surveys to the proper officials, discussed possibilities, and signed some agreements. Now Matt was ready to visit Parker again.

Parker, a much larger man, started to throw Matt out of his office. However, something in the soldier's eyes caused Parker to have second thoughts about that course of action. In the same manner he had used during their first encounter, Matt showed the man a map of the timber tracts Parker's company was harvesting. Only one road led to Parker's mill from these tracts, and on this one road was a bridge.

Matt went on to explain that this bridge had been condemned by the county. The county government did not have any money in the coffers to build a new bridge, so Matt had worked out a deal with county officials. Matt would build a new bridge, and in exchange the county would allow him to charge a toll. Cars would cross for five cents, but trucks would be charged $1.00 a ton. As logs are quite heavy, Parker saw immediately that he would pay dearly!

Everything was legal. Matt had done his homework, taken the necessary precautions, and dotted each *i*. Matt now made a deal with Parker. "You play fair with Dad, and I'll waive the toll for trucks. Otherwise, we'll collect more from the toll bridge than we'll ever make from the lumber mill."

Parker was defeated, and Matt Wiley, the mountain-boy soldier, had done it his own way.

Nero and Jethro

Some of the folks around here love to tell about Nero and Jethro—and I love to hear them talk about these young men of a few decades past. These twins from the Southern Highlands never had much formal education, but they were somehow accepted into the ninth grade.

On the first day of school in 1950, they shyly slipped into the classroom as their fellow students rushed to get the choice seats in the back of the room. Nero and Jethro hesitated just inside the door, looking around in a bewildered way, and then slid into two empty front-row seats near the room's entrance. The other students continued to buzz, but the twins sat like statues, wide-eyed, as they stared at their surroundings and at the teacher writing her name on the blackboard. They held tightly to dime-store tablets and pencils. Nero and Jethro had stepped into a new world.

As the days and weeks went by, the twins remained quiet. While in class, they never whispered to anyone, and no one whispered to them. They struggled through English, had trouble with math, and were confused by geography and general science. In all their classes, they either stared blankly at the teachers or bent laboriously over the work at hand. With pencils clutched tightly, they would work hour after hour to produce papers covered with mistake upon mistake.

The entire freshman class was rather slow, but Nero and

Jethro were the slowest by far. Teachers scolded the boys about their lessons occasionally, and they would look up at the teachers with remorse in their eyes, their mouths drawn into masks of guilty grief. "We'uns's sorry we's so dumb," Jethro told one of the teachers after a scolding. She looked at him, bit her lip, slightly shook her head, and smiled. Then Jethro smiled and Nero followed, like two little puppies trying to make up with their master.

Soon, all the teachers began to walk the extra mile to help the twins and encourage them. If the twins happened to get two of ten test questions correct, more than likely the teacher would write on the paper "Good! You got two of them right," rather than focusing on the ones they had gotten wrong. One day, a teacher found one of Jethro's papers with her written comment neatly removed. She questioned Jethro about it. "We'uns saves 'em," Jethro said shyly. "Mama pastes 'em in a big book. She's awful proud of all the nice things written to us."

The other students shunned Nero and Jethro. They were their own companions. Each day, they brought their lunches and sat alone, eating their plain meals from a paper sack while the other children ate and talked noisily in the lunchroom. Nero and Jethro would sit watching the antics of the students with eager interest and delight, whispering to each other, chuckling every now and then at whatever pleased them, but never being offered nor ever offering to join in the fun.

In the spring, it came time to have the annual freshman party. The students voted to charge twenty-five cents a ticket to pay for some food and drinks at the party, and to have dancing and a talent show. The next day after school, Miss Martin, the twins' homeroom teacher, was correcting some test papers when the door to her room opened and the twins quietly strolled in.

Jethro's face turned red as he approached the teacher's desk. She asked the twins what she could do for them. Jethro looked back toward his brother, who remained near the door. He motioned for Nero to come on up, and the boy joined him in front of the teacher's desk. Again, Miss Martin asked what she might do for them.

"We'uns's got gittars," Jethro answered softly.

"Paw helpt us make 'em 'fore he died," Nero added.

"We'uns make music and sing songs," Jethro came back.

Miss Martin looked at them and their expectant faces. "That's nice," she responded. Then there was silence. Studying their expressions, Miss Martin was at a loss for words. Their eyes begged her to say something, but she could not imagine what. It didn't occur to her that the two boys would want to perform in the talent show.

Jethro broke the silence. "But we'uns ain't got no quarters," he said, his mouth drooping sadly.

"We'll work for you, Miss Martin," Nero suggested.

"Like cleaning the blackboards extra good and sweeping the floor and tending the stove," Jethro jumped in with his prepared proposal.

"That sounds fine," Miss Martin quickly responded as things finally began to make sense to her.

The day of the party neared, and excitement began to run high in the freshman class. Even though no one paid any attention to the fact that the twins were going to be on the program, the two boys whispered to Miss Martin that they had been "practicin' up."

The big day arrived. The party was to begin at seven, and at six-thirty that evening the gym was almost filled with students. Girls in brand-new party dresses, with their hair in curls, sat on one side of the decorated gym. Boys, dressed uncomfortably in Sunday clothes and shoes, with their damp hair brushed down, were seated on the opposite side.

The talent show was first on the agenda. The program got underway promptly. A couple of tap dancers started things off, but the response to their act was far from terrific. Some of the boys accused the two girls of trying to step on roaches while music played. Next came a soloist, who went through two songs and an unwanted encore and never did find the right key. This performance was followed by some poetry reading, mumbled by a student who didn't dare to look into the audience. An excruciating violin solo followed. Next, an instrumental group livened things up a bit, and a quartet did a commendable job.

The twins then came out to close the show and free the crowd for dancing and eating. When introduced, they hesitated, looking dwarfed and lonely under the specially prepared homemade floodlights. Their faces showed fear as they clutched their cheap "gittars" close to their ill-fitting Sunday-best clothes.

Nero and Jethro struck a few chords and began to sing. The crowd went wild. They had never heard a beat and a harmony like Nero and Jethro shared that evening. When the first number ended, people whistled and stamped their feet. The audience cheered the twins on, and they kept playing and singing, song after song.

Nero and Jethro played and sang as the class danced. They performed while the food was distributed. The class president himself brought them two heaped plates and clapped each boy on the back, congratulating them for making the party a huge success. The boys never left the stage the rest of the evening. The record player that had been brought to play dance music was never plugged in. Once again, Nero and Jethro had stepped into another new world.

Mountain Aristocrats

In 1935, Marjorie Chalmers came to Gatlinburg to serve for a year as the nurse at the Pi Beta Phi Settlement School and in the community. After devoting thirty years of service to the people of Gatlinburg and the surrounding area, she finally retired here in 1965. Following her retirement, she often spoke about her experiences, always with an admiration for the isolated mountaineers who responded with kindness as she went the extra mile to assist them in any way she could.

Marjorie loved the mountain people, and they loved her. "Aristocrats they are," Marjorie said, talking about the "true hill folk of the area." She claimed, "They hold within themselves a poise and an innate courtesy." Whenever she was in their homes, even in her early years when she was still a "furriner," they treated her as an honored guest. "I was always welcomed to the best they had," she said. "It might have been an unfinished, straight-back chair, but it was offered graciously and 'hit set good.' At meals, there might not have been a large variety on the table, but I was told to 'reach out and take yore needs.'"

Marjorie described most of the men as quiet and dignified. She said they were so quiet that, until you got to know them, you could not appreciate their keen minds and great humor. She said, "The womenfolk had the serene poise of the hills. They may have been ever so interested in me, but if they finally came to the point of questioning, it was done in friendly fashion."

Marjorie was impressed that greetings to the smallest children even brought forth a mannerly reply. "Even the babies were friendly," she claimed. "Give them a few moments to look you over, speaking and moving quietly, and they would usually come to you willingly, with the mother often remarking pridefully, 'Hit ain't scared a mite. Hit never sees a stranger.'" Marjorie smiled when she said, "What an expressive way to say that all who come are looked upon as friends."

Despite the many superstitions and mountain remedies she had to overcome in order to help, she said these mountaineers possessed a wealth of knowledge that transcended mere book learning. Marjorie understood that the mountaineers' relatives left the Old World and came to America in search of religious freedom and independence. In the mountains of East Tennessee they found it, fought to keep it, and endured the privations and adventures of true pioneers to sustain it.

"Independent they were," she said, describing those pioneers, "and they were deeply religious." The independence and religion were evident in the lives of the current generation when Marjorie arrived in 1935.

"Why shouldn't they be proud?" she said. "In this broad land of ours, there are none with better heritage. In their veins flow the blood of men and women of distinction, people who had the courage of their convictions and the strength of body and soul to suffer, if need be, for their ideals."

From the time of the American Revolution and up until only a couple of generations ago, the people of the Great Smoky Mountains were almost totally isolated in the practically impassible wilderness. "That isolation," Marjorie claimed, "may have been a blessing in disguise. At least, it seems so to us who have come to know them."

Marjorie commented on how the isolated people brought to others much of the best of the days gone by, that their speech still had an Old World flavor, and that many of the folk songs and folkways of earlier days had, to a certain degree, survived.

"It was a new world to me," Marjorie said. She came from a city hospital in the North, and she thought the little village of Gatlinburg, the narrow valley beside the river, the heavily wooded hills, and the steep, winding trails "were sheer beauty." Marjorie appreciated the beauty of the mountaineers even more than the beauty of the area.

Near the end of her life, Marjorie reflected on the change that had taken place in Gatlinburg. Once a sleepy little mountain village, it had become the most visited mountain resort in America, with over eleven million tourists a year viewing the beauty of the Great Smoky Mountains National Park.

According to Marjorie, "I still feel the butterflies in my stomach when I think of the first time I ever crossed a footlog laid high above a mountain stream. I was so certain my heavy 'doctorin' bag' would pull me sideways into the water. Only the suspicion that someone in the cabin across the creek was watching my hesitation forced my unwilling feet onto the plank.

"I remember, too, the times I pulled red coals forward onto the hearth, balancing a basin atop to boil instruments or heat a compress. How many times I stood beside a bed, helping the doctor while some father's shaking hand held the big flashlight, smiling at the irate wail of a minute-old baby.

"There were some wild car rides with frequent blasts of the horn, where a few minutes meant the difference between life and death. One such ride was with a child who had been bitten by a copperhead snake. It took fifty minutes to get from her house to the doctor's office in Knoxville. Over the old winding road we bounced, as her sister used a suction cup to delay the rush of the poison in order that the doctor would have a chance to save her. She was saved, and how thankful I was that the boys at the garage took such excellent care of my car in order that such trips could be made.

"That old car had many strange duties. It carried armloads

of laurel and rhododendron to dress the church for a wedding. It transported groceries, clothing, and coal all over the mountains. It took sick children from school or to the hospital. It brought new babies to their homes.

"Once, it was a hearse. A very young baby who lived up in the area called Forks of the River had died. There was no burial insurance and no money in the family. To me, the thought of a rough pine box for this precious little baby was awful. So into Sevierville we went and purchased a tiny white coffin lined with silk. The baby was dressed in dainty new things. Flowers from the garden made a wee blanket.

"Carefully, the coffin was set on the back seat of the car. Two little sisters crowded in beside it, with more flowers in their hands. The mother and her sister got into the front seat with me. Followed by a pickup truck carrying the rest of the family, we slowly drove over the rough road to a little cemetery.

"There was no preacher. But the family told me that the verses of Scripture I read were comforting. Simple, but comforting. To officiate at the funeral of one whom you have helped to bring into this world, and have cared for in health and in sickness, is to run the full gamut of emotion.

"The years have been overflowing. The work, at times, was overly hard. But they have been good years, with the knowledge of a little accomplished to make things a bit easier for some folk. There has been a blessing of many friends—generous, warmhearted friends—who have never been found wanting.

"There has been the joy of living in one of nature's beauty spots. I have lifted mine eyes to the hills over and over again, and found inspiration and strength and peace of soul."

Marjorie Chalmers is now absent from the body and present with the Lord. But her spirit permeates the mountains in and around a tiny little hamlet that has become a tourist mecca. "Miss Marjorie," as she was called by many of her patients and friends, was a true Mountain Aristocrat.

Acknowledgments and Notes

Special thanks to: Carolyn Sakowski for recommending me to Beth Wright, my publisher; Beth for inviting me to send the *People of Passion* manuscript; Daniel Lewis, managing editor, with whom I worked during the editorial reading process and beyond; Jason Weems, my editor, who spent hours and hours working with me on the manuscript to get the product we all desired; Bill May, Jr. for designing the cover and incorporating Vern Hippensteal's original painting; all the other valuable personnel at The Overmountain Press who contribute to the teamwork; and my wife, Jean, for always supporting and affirming me.

Some of the stories herein are little known; others have been circulated orally and/or in some type of written form. At times, I drew from several versions of the same account and, with editing, wrote what I believed to be the truest, most succinct version. Along with the elderly area residents I interviewed in the 1970s, I consulted with historians and others who were knowledgeable of the Appalachian Mountains and her people.

Most of the interviewees have passed away. Most of the historians and others from whom I gleaned information have either passed away or have been long retired. Thus, I feel it is important to give recognition to the following individuals and sources that inspired me and originally pointed me toward the interviewees and toward a better understanding of the Southern Highlands, helping me write the stories and history found in *People of Passion*.

- **Anna Porter Public Library, Gatlinburg, Tennessee**—All libraries are valuable community resources. In my quest to uncover, write, and compile the material now found in *People of Passion*, the Anna Porter Public Library proved to be of special value. Its Smoky Mountains Collection, an in-house reference section, provides journals, taped interviews, genealogies, and other resources that serve as a gold mine for anyone wanting to know more about the Southern Highlands and her people. Verla King, Vertie Sharp, and June Watson were instrumental in guiding me through the stacks in the 1970s and directing me toward some elderly people who could spin a tale. Guiding people at the library today are Kenton Temple, Betty Webb, and Autumn Davis.
- **Boykin, Shirley McHan**—In the 1970s, Ms. Boykin was the executive director of the Great Smoky Mountains Natural History Association, an organization formed to complement the work of the National Park Service. Ms. Boykin's job was to help people realize and appreciate not only the natural beauty and history of the Great Smoky Mountains National Park (GSMNP), but also to learn more about the area's human heritage. A division was established to facilitate home economists and others who "interpreted" how the early inhabitants of the area lived. I was invited to speak to and for the organization. These were times of learning for me. Today, this organization is known as the Great Smoky Mountains Association, with Terry Maddox serving as executive director.
- **Brewer, Carson**—A journalist for the *Knoxville News-*

Sentinel, author, storyteller, and hiker, Mr. Brewer was an expert on the Great Smoky Mountains, their trails, and their residents. Not only did he introduce me to some human resources, he also pointed me toward some passed-along tales, history, and geography lessons from chroniclers such as Horace Kephart, Michael Frome, Harvey Broome, and others. I shouldn't have been surprised, however, that some of the elderly interviewees shared with me information and stories similar to that of these chroniclers but had never heard of the writers who documented them. It reminded me of the question, Where and by whom do jokes begin? While gathering tales, I wondered, Where and by whom do stories and tales begin?

- **Campbell, Carlos**—In the 1920s and 1930s, Mr. Campbell worked hard to help establish the GSMNP. And even though it displeased some mountain residents (such as the Walker sisters), the GSMNP became a reality in 1934. When Franklin D. Roosevelt eventually dedicated the park on September 2, 1940, Mr. Campbell was there to file a written report on the event. He was the president of the Knoxville Chamber of Commerce in the 1920s, and he constantly worked to unite the city and her people with the mountains and her people. He was still heavily involved in these endeavors in the 1970s and on into the 1980s. And, Mr. Campbell knew many people. His treasury of names led me to some wonderful, beautiful people and their stories.

- **Cardwell, Glen**—A native of Sevier County, Tennessee, and a longtime friend, Glen was a ranger and communications specialist at the GSMNP. He served the Great Smoky Mountains Natural History Association, speaking to groups about the early Cherokees, mountaineers, and highlanders. Having been retired from the National Park Service for a number of years now, at this writing Glen capably serves as the mayor of Pittman Center, a small community dedicated to preserving the area's heritage. While with the

GSMNP, he asked me to speak to some of the organization's groups, and he enlisted me to record the vehicle tour information that visitors heard when tuning to certain frequencies on their radio dial. As a result, I became quite familiar with the expansive park and surrounding areas, as well as with the inhabitants.

- **Chalmers, Marjorie**—The last story in this book, "Mountain Aristocrats," is a brief tribute to a fruitful life, given in service to the residents of Gatlinburg and Sevier County, Tennessee. From 1935-1965, Miss Chalmers "birthed, nursed, and buried" the hill folk, as she earned her way into their lives and hearts. I first met Miss Chalmers when she spoke of her work at a community gathering. While talking with her afterward, she pointed me toward some possible interviewees and proved to be a great one herself. She also showed interest in a couple of my published books, which she had read. Later, Blanche McCarter, co-owner (with her husband Bill) of Gatlinburg's Crescent Color Printing Company, contacted me to say, "Marjorie wants to know if you will help her to put her story in book form." Her seventy-one-page story, *Better I Stay*, was printed in 1975.

- **Clabo, Herb**—As of this writing, Herb is one of the few contributors to this book that is still alive. I saw him just the other day in a local bank, in bib overalls, still spry and full of tales about the Great Smoky Mountains. Craig McCarter, son of Crescent Color Printing's Bill and Blanche McCarter, constantly prodded Herb into telling story after story of "how it used to be." Born in 1911, Herb watched Gatlinburg grow from a tiny mountain village to a flourishing resort town. As a young man, he was proud he got to work "off and on" at the sawmill for ten cents an hour. He was also glad to tell me, "You oughta ast ole so and so," about something. Often, I did.

- **Evison, Boyd**—Mr. Evison was superintendent of the

GSMNP for only a few years, 1975-1978, but he is still remembered for the work he accomplished. He is especially known for creating the park's system of short, easy walking trails referred to as "quiet walkways." These trails offer visitors a chance to get out of their vehicles and into the environment for at least a brief experience. Mr. Evison was happy to share with me his books and the park's library regarding the history of the National Park Service and, especially, the history of the Appalachian Mountains.

- **Great Smoky Mountains Association**—This nonprofit organization was founded in 1953. Its purpose is to help the National Park Service fulfill its mission by providing various tools through volunteer efforts, labor, donations, and merchandise sales. The organization helps to interpret the botanical, animal, and human heritage of the area. I've had the opportunity to work with this group, and I fondly remember speaking at an annual board dinner meeting when Carson Brewer was a member. Today, the organization works closely with other nonprofit groups that have formed to aid the National Park Service in its mission. These groups include: Friends Of The Great Smoky Mountains National Park; Gateway Gatlinburg Association; Great Smoky Mountain Institute at Tremont; Appalachian Bear Center; Cradle of Forestry; Discover Life in America; and Foothills Land Conservatory.

- **Heard, Marian**—Marian served as director of Arrowmont School of Arts and Crafts in Gatlinburg from 1945 through 1977. Under her leadership, the school was begun and developed into one that reached out to educators, craftspeople, and students from around the world. Meanwhile, she made a significant contribution to the local economy and educational advancement. She believed strongly in the value of people and the value of crafts. Marian was born in 1908 in Boswell's Corners, New York. After receiving her graduate degree from Columbia University Teachers College in New York City, she taught at the University of Tennessee from 1936-1977. She was always ready to share stories about the Appalachian people and to praise them for their achievements under trying circumstances.

- **Hippensteal, Vern**—Vern has been featured in American Artist's *Watercolor*, the country's leading magazine on fine art. He is a renowned artist whose work is displayed in his Gatlinburg gallery and in galleries and homes across America and the world. His beautiful paintings also adorn Hippensteal's Mountain View Inn, an acclaimed bed and breakfast in the Great Smoky Mountains where Vern is artist-in-residence. A Gatlinburg native, his transparent watercolors portray the visual splendor of the mountains and their timelessness. Friends for many years, I asked Vern about the possibility of using one of his prints as the cover for *People of Passion*. In response, he suggested a new original painting for the cover. I was elated. The result is a painting titled *Smoky Mountain Passion*. He intends for this painting to become the first in his new Giclée Collection. For more information on Vern and his work, you may visit his Web site, www.hippenstealgallery.com.

- **Linn, Beulah**—After attending high school in Knoxville, acquiring an undergraduate degree at Maryville College, then a graduate degree at the University of Tennessee, Miss Linn began teaching at Gatlinburg's Pi Beta Phi Settlement School in 1954. After three years, she left to attend the Baptist Hospital School of Nursing. Receiving her accreditation, Miss Linn returned to Pi Beta Phi, where she taught for many years. Later, she became known as "Sevier County Historian," chronicling the families and occurrences of the county. Anyone wanting to learn how to trace genealogies and specific events could go to Miss Linn for assistance, and she was willing to help. She led in the promotion of the History and Genealogy Center at the Sevier County Public Library in Sevierville, Tennessee. The more recently established Pigeon Forge Public Library in Pigeon Forge, Tennessee, learned the importance of featuring a strong regional section from the Sevier County Public Library and the Anna Porter Public Library.

- **Maples, Wilma**—Born in Union County, Tennessee, Mrs. Maples attended Knoxville Business College and began working for an insurance company, but she didn't like the work. She contacted the college and asked them to notify her of any openings they thought might interest her. As a result, in 1943 she received a war-service appointment to work with the Great Smoky Mountains National Park. She moved to Gatlinburg and became secretary for John Needham, chief park ranger. When the temporary appointment ended, she was hired by Rel Maples, founder of the Gatlinburg Inn, to work during the summers.

  At age twenty-seven, after five years of this part-time work, Wilma decided to find something more permanent, and she moved to Oak Ridge for a job. Three years later, out of the blue, she was bowled over when she received a letter from Rel Maples, asking her to marry him. She told me that she never prayed over anything in her life as much as she prayed about this. She was thirty and he was forty-eight when they married. At this writing, Rel has passed away, but Mrs. Maples still manages the Gatlinburg Inn. She is a tremendous source of stories about the area, and we have made plans to work on a book to make sure many more of her stories are recorded.

- **Oakley, Casey**—I could write a book about Casey Oakley. Maybe one day I will. He is definitely one of a kind. Often, I have told people that Willie Nelson looks like Casey, because Casey had the look—bandanna and all—long before Willie shed his coat and tie. Casey is a son of the renowned Wiley Oakley. When I met Casey in the early 1970s, he was living in a tent alongside the Greenbrier River. This was his abode for many years. More recently, however, due to arthritis and other maladies, he has moved from the tent by the river into a small trailer in a campground.

From Casey, I learned of his father. He showed me some journals and guided me through a thirty-six-page booklet titled *The Roamin' Man Of The Mountains: A Sketch by Edna Lynn Simms*, printed in 1940. Later, a booklet of a similar nature was self-published by Wiley, followed by another booklet, *Restin'*. After Wiley died in 1954 and his wife Rebecca Ann died in the 1980s, the two booklets were combined into one volume. It has been updated a couple of times by Wiley's son, Harvey, and Harvey's wife, Melba.

The Smoky Mountains Collection of the Anna Porter Public Library has a taped interview with Wiley, Rebecca Ann, and their daughter, Martha Oakley Rawlings. The National Park Service, with Jane Whitney serving as interviewer, produced the tape and the printed transcript in 1954, shortly before Wiley died of cancer. Wiley and Rebecca Ann's other children include Elmer, Woodrow, Orville, and Lucinda Oakley Ogle. They also have been great preservers of the area's heritage. Even within the last few years, Lucinda has made the front pages of newspapers, depicted in photos and stories about shooing bears out of her mountain-home kitchen with a broom. It seems the bears can't resist her cooking!

- **Purkey, Lena Penland**—As my stories appeared in several newspapers and magazines in the 1970s and on into the 1980s, I received numerous letters, along with family stories shared by some of the letter writers. That's how I came to know Ms. Purkey, who wrote me from Morristown, Tennessee, telling me that she was "born and bred" in the Mountains of East Tennessee (Cocke County) and Western North Carolina (Madison County). She told me that she enjoyed my stories in the *Newport Plain Talk* (Cocke County) newspaper and that they brought back memories, and she asked if I might be interested in sharing some of her personal experiences. She also sent me some handwritten and printed copies of some other stories she had gathered. *People of Passion* contains three of her personal accounts, and I did use portions of the other material she sent to me.

- **Taylor, Chief Jonathan L.**—In 1976, this Cherokee chief and some tribal officials regained possession of over three and a half acres of land from Kingsport, Tennessee. The Cherokee Nation had held the land years earlier. Apart from trying to regain physical and material losses, Chief Taylor worked to help his people regain cultural pride. He introduced me to the Cherokee Historical Association and the Oconaluftee Living Indian Village. He filled me in on some Cherokee history and led me to meet such artisans as sculptor John J. Wilnoty and basket maker Rowena Bradley. In the 1970s, these role models inspired young Cherokees to feel proud of their heritage and to learn the art for themselves.
- **Terrell, Bob**—A journalist and storyteller from Western North Carolina, Mr. Terrell was, through his grandfather, acquainted with many elderly people who loved to sit and talk about days gone by. He was open to sharing his stories and contacts with anyone who wanted to learn about the Southern Highlanders and chronicle their tales. Mr. Terrell was especially interested in rural churches in the late 1800s and early 1900s. He claimed, "The religion of the time still contained a portion of the hypocrisy of the Dark Ages, with its light still partially shuttered beneath the bushel." However, he also emphasized that without religion and without the rural churches, the Appalachian culture would not have become as strong as it did.
- **Trotter, Jim, Jr.**—Jim was the editor at the *Gatlinburg Press* in the 1970s, the paper, along with the *Sevier County News-Record*, that first published my "Stories from the Smokies" as a weekly column. (These two papers later became known as the *Mountain Press*.) Jim encouraged me to submit the

column to other papers and magazines, which I did. Born and reared in Gatlinburg, Jim has been a much read journalist. Writing for the *Austin American-Statesman*, he covered the Dallas Cowboys in their glory days under Tom Landry. He was a columnist for the *Sacramento Bee*, spent many years as a columnist for the *San Jose Mercury News*, and currently writes and edits for Denver's *Rocky Mountain News*.

- *Camping in the Smokies* **and** *Our Smokies Heritage*—A special note goes to these two publications, the first magazines to carry my "Stories from the Smokies" column after it had appeared in regional newspapers. Begun by Crescent Color Printing Company, these monthly magazines were popular in the 1970s and 1980s. Initially introduced and distributed through campgrounds, motels, hotels, shops, restaurants, and entertainment venues, they soon built a large following and a list of subscribers. Each issue contained at least one of my stories and also one of my philosophical columns titled "Reaching Out—Touching Life." Credit goes to Bill and Blanche McCarter for founding the publications; to renowned artist Vern Hippensteal for helping to make the periodicals extremely attractive; and to Mary Schultz, Tom Whitted, and the entire staff for turning out a polished product each month. Terri McCarter Waters, daughter of Bill and Blanche, heads up the printing company today.

An effort has been made not to use any material in this book for which proper credit has not been given or permission granted. Since *People of Passion* is a compilation of some of the columns and articles I wrote in the 1970s and is comprised of historical research and oral and written material passed along to me and edited by me, I have relied on the interviewees, other sources, and myself for authenticity. If any error or omission has occurred, it is inadvertent, and I would like to make corrections in future editions of this book, provided that written, documented notification is sent to me at P.O. Box 808, Gatlinburg, TN 37738.

Also, if you wish to contribute stories and/or historical material to a sequel to *People of Passion*, please contact me at the above address or at People-of-Passion@CarlMays.com.

About the Author

Carl Mays has authored a dozen books, seven dramas, and three newspaper columns. He is a professional speaker and consultant who deals with human relations, inspiration, and self-improvement. He has spoken to over 2500 groups, and is a recipient of the National Speakers Association's Certified Speaking Professional and Council of Peers Award for Excellence designations. He is a member of the Speaker Hall of Fame.

Born and reared in Humboldt, Tennessee, Carl obtained his undergraduate degree from Kentucky's Murray State University, where, in 1990, he received the Distinguished Alumnus Award. He earned his graduate degree from New Orleans Baptist Seminary, and did additional work at the University of Memphis.

Carl was the founder of a successful conference sales group in Gatlinburg, Tennessee, and was the charter chairman of the Gatlinburg Board of Education. He has served the city and county in numerous ways and is one of the area's best goodwill ambassadors. Carl and his wife, Jean, have been residents of Gatlinburg since 1972. They have one son, Carl Mays II, who lives with his wife, Beth, and son, Carl Mays III (Trey), in Texas.

Carl may be contacted at P.O. Box 808, Gatlinburg, TN 37738 or by E-mail at carlmays@carlmays.com. Visit his Web site at www.carlmays.com.